Dynamics
of
Marriage

...grounding for happier and stronger marriage

Dynamics of Marriage

"THE FAMILY OF ORIGIN" APPROACH

— *Workbook* —

Leticia S. Isidro-Clancy

STONEWALL PRESS

PAVING YOUR WAY TO SUCCESS

Published in the United States of America

ISBN: 978-1-64460-009-2 (*sc*)
   978-1-64460-008-5 (*e*)

Library of Congress Control Number: 2018957819

Published by Stonewall Press
4800 Hampden Lane, Suite 200, Bethesda, MD 20814 USA
1.888.334.0980 | www.stonewallpress.com

1. Family
2. Guide
3. Self-Help

18.09.25

CONTENTS

PRAISE FOR THE DYNAMICS OF MARRIAGE: "THE FAMILY OF ORIGIN" APPROACH

Marital and Family counseling can be arduous work for even the most experienced clinician. The Dynamics of Marriage: "The Family of Origin" Approach Workbook makes the work easier and more enjoyable. The author, Leticia Isidro-Clancy, has crafted a text that is succinct yet extremely informative. The added form helps communicate difficult concepts to the patient(s) and promotes insight on part of each family member. Congrats on a job well done!

—Kasi Patterson, PhD

The Dynamics of Marriage: "The Family of Origin" Approach Workbook is filled with helpful techniques and easy to understand guide to help couples find their way back to each other. I believe this manual crosses all faith, race, gender barriers that sometimes prevent success in marriage from taking place. Although nothing is ever guaranteed, it is great to know that if a couple is serious about repairing their marriage, or serious about helping their marriage stay strong, they will take the time to use this manual that can help them reach their goal.

—Natalie Milligan, LCSW

The author demonstrates excellent skill in turning complex concepts into practical exercises for persons in committed relationships. By engaging in the exercises presented in this book couples will have an opportunity to explore the interplay between the family of origin experience and the dynamics of the current relationship. This tool is a powerful tool for growing as an individual within a committed relationship; thus making the foundation of the relationship stronger! Whether you believe your relationship is struggling, or you would simply like to explore the core of the dynamics in your relationship, this is a must read for increasing and improving the bond between partners!!!!

—Nena

ACKNOWLEDGMENTS

To MY PARENTS ANDRES and Veronica Salo Isidro, who carried out their responsibilities as parents, and unwittingly taught me so many dominant lessons in life and the importance of relationships.

To my six siblings, who epitomized the multivalent variations of self-development coming from within my family. You taught me respect for and acceptance of the evershifting differences that abound in people.

To my husband, Marty, for his loving and continued support. He is also my most objective critics. He epitomizes the importance of a collaborating partner in a growing marriage.

To my children, Ligaya and Lee Martin, for their ever-continuing support, their loving presence in my life. They continue their manifest affirmation of who I am. Your living legacy is the value possible in all relationships.

My personal and professional gratitude goes to the many couples that I have worked with. Thank you, couple-friends, for sharing your families of origin lessons; the lessons of your hard-won experience continuously prompt and confirm my observations and on-going work.

This manuscript would never have come into being without these pioneers in the work of the family of origin, Murray Bowen and Ivan Bonzormenyi-Nagy, James L. Framo, and Susan Forward. Also, to Ronald Richardson for his Family Ties that Bind. For this book, I owe many thanks to my friend, Carmen Gaston, for her critical input on the workbook exercises, and to Jane Fitzgerald for her valuable critique on the relevancy of the workbook. Most of all I owe my son, Lee, many thanks for his hard work in editing the draft of this book.

BRIEF SYNOPSIS

DYNAMICS OF MARRIAGE: "THE Family of Origin" Approach is a unique way of doing therapy with couples. It brings awareness to the participating couples how they are shaped by their family of origin, and how this is impacting their relationship with their spouse and other members of the family. This knowledge could lead to taking ownership of the problems they bring into the marriage, and therefore the changes that need to be made. The therapeutic style create an open and accepting environment which encourages honesty and truthfulness, while exploring maybe painful past experiences of the family of origin.

The manual provides guideline to avoid repeating destructive patterns of behavior that will destroy the marriage. Or, it makes them aware of the behaviors that bind the couple in maintaining the equilibrium of the marriage and the status quo of the relationship unproductively.

This workbook is a tool in processing the work of a growing marriage. This growth requires investigation of and re-discovery of the person. As individual awareness develops, the level of trust between partners will allow the risk of candid openness. As each couple progresses, they will realized the influence that the Family of Origin contributes to the problems in the relationship. This phenomenon is universal, multigenerational and generally unrecognized. In many cases, it is the underlying cause when a marriage falters or fails.

FOREWORD

THE DYNAMICS OF MARRIAGE: "The Family of Origin" Approach is a workbook, a tool in processing the work of a growing marriage.

This workbook allows motivated individuals in relationships to identify their issues with or without the help of a therapist. However, if in the process of working this program one or both partners find that there are personal issues interfering in their individual growth, and the growth of the marriage, it is highly recommended that they take responsibility to seek help from a professional.

It takes honesty with oneself and motivation to admit this. It is possible that an individual may lose his/her objectivity in truly understanding the impact of their family of origin.

Any feedback or discussion from the spouse might be met with resistance and would fall on deaf ears. The loss of objectivity could be due to being entrenched in his/her family system. The individual perceives the dynamics of the family of origin as "being normal." Or, it could be due to a strong, and needed, denial system. If personal issues are not addressed prior or concomitant with the couple's work, the likelihood of achieving any change in the relationship will not happen. It is the prerogative of each person to change or not to change. Each one has the responsibility to make a choice to live or not in the "status quo" of the relationship. The choice may inevitably result is the termination of the marriage, but even deeper—in self-destructive decision-making.

The topics of this workbook are divided in progression into thirteen Chapters. 1) Assessment of the status of my marriage 2) The assessment of my marriage skills and its bases; 3) Communication, 4) The accountability I bring to my marriage; 5) Reacquainting myself with my past experiences through the genogram; 6) Understanding the legacy of my family of origin; 7) Learning more about me in the context of my marriage; 8) Uniqueness of each marriage; 9) Multidimensional aspects of my marriage; 10) Moving forward on my marriage; 11) Keeping the commitment alive; 12) My marriage: preventing the return of my old behaviors; 13) Re-evaluating the foundations of the strength of my marriage.

INTRODUCTION

The *Dynamics of Marriage: "The Family of Origin" Approach Workbook* is a vital tool in processing the work of a growing marriage. Growth requires investigation of, and rediscovery of the person. As the individual awareness develops, the level of trust between partners will allow the risk of candid openness.

As each couple progresses, they will realize how the influence of their Families of Origin (FOO) contributes to the problems in their relationship. This phenomenon is universal, multi-generational and generally unrecognized. In many cases, it is the underlying cause when a marriage falters.

The purpose of examining our Family of Origin is not to blame our parents, but to develop an understanding of the impact of FOO, and to effect change within our marriage and ourselves. Without this awareness and acceptance, healing and becoming an integrated person is not possible.

TO THE THERAPIST

You will bring your expertise using different therapeutic approaches in processing the material the couple brings to therapy. The workbook will help serve as a guide and an aide in your work with couples.

The premise is that couples are experts in their marriage. From the beginning they know what they want from their marriage. However, in their journey as a couple many lose their unified direction toward an enriching and productive partnership. They need guidelines and structure to help them articulate their problems. Following this workbook will guide the couple through their confusion within their own hard-won expertise. It will instill hope and faith to recreate their marriage.

*The best therapist cannot lead an individual unless that individual wishes to grow and are willing to follow instructions."

THE ROLE OF A THERAPIST

The central interest of the therapist is to guide the couple in improving their communication. Consequently, the therapist enables the couple to a better understanding of each other, and to improve their interpersonal relationship skills. The therapist acts as a "third listening ear" in:

- helping the couple to understand and overcome errors in thinking (cognitive distortions)
- helping the couple to establish boundaries
- helping the couple to clarify issues

TO THE COUPLE

Dynamics of Marriage: "The Family of Origin" Approach is purposefully easy to understand and easy to follow. It will indirectly help couples to define the persistent and chronic problems that invade relationships with their repetitive themes. Consequently, every couple could initiate the work on their marriage using the movements and exercises in this workbook as a guide. Predictably, one may wonder if any of these recurring problems can ever be resolved.

The answer is a resounding yes! In the course of the work and in following the guidelines/exercises individually or as a couple, one may feel that the "real problems" in the marriage are not being addressed. However, these exercises, based on how we were shaped by our Family of Origins, will reveal that both individuals have the capacity to reach for and achieve better understandings of themselves, of their behaviors, and their mutual and individual feelings and thinking processes.

The couple will recognize that a particular marital conflict affords them the opportunity to understand the reason for the issue that stands between them. With this understanding, each person will gain insights into their behaviors and thought processes, and realize they are exhibiting groundless behavior in their present situation.

By learning about yourself and what is important in your marriage, any conflict that may arise in the future will be handled with greater clarity of purpose and, therefore, with more confidence. Conversely, without this understanding, it will be difficult to convey the importance of what you believe, as well as what your spouse believes in.

As a result, both you and your spouse will continue to fight blindly for what you both want.

The practice in self-discovery through the exercises in this workbook will equip both spouses with the skills and self-knowledge they need. Therefore, whatever the issues maybe, both will be able to discuss them with well-grounded reasons, keeping always in the forefront that the goal is the growth of their marriage.

All the predictable and painful difficulties arising within this process to which you have committed yourselves might help you realize the need for the guidance and the experience of a chosen therapist. This person can help you navigate unknown waters, and will empower you both with your own experience and history as a couple and as an individual. Working together with a therapist will spotlight the irreplaceable necessity for honesty and generous, and a willingness in confronting marital issues. This will help both spouses strengthen their commitment to their marriage.

There is a timeless proverb that provides truths and long-accepted realities: *"Give a man a fish and you feed him for a day. Teach him to fish and you feed him for the rest of his life."* When you solve just one problem through a hard-won understanding of its deeper cause within you, you will look back and know what it means to say, *"You've just been spinning your wheels."*

For Marriage Preparation Sessions

The following chapters of this workbook can also be adapted to function within the perspectives of a couple anticipating marriage. In place of the word marriage uses the word relationship.

Introduction

> Chapter 1: Assessment of the status of my marriage
>
> Chapter 2: Assessment of my marriage skills and its bases (Pre & Post screening)
>
> Chapter 3: Communication
>
> Chapter 4: The accountability I bring to my marriage
>
> Chapter 5: Reacquainting myself with my past experiences through genogram
>
> Chapter 6: Understanding the legacy of my family of origin
>
> Chapter 7: Learning more about me in the context of my marriage.

SEQUENCE/PROGRESSION OF DYNAMICS OF MARRIAGE: "THE FAMILY OF ORIGIN" APPROACH

This workbook, Dynamics of Marriage: "The Family of Origin" Approach, provides a stepby-step process of understanding the work that needs to be done for individual growth in the marriage and also of the marriage itself.

The parts of the book are progressive—from starting with what attracted the couple to each other, on to assessing the cause of the foreseeable breakdown of their relationship, to mending and maintaining their marriage.

- Chapter 1 to 4—Allow the couple to re-evaluate and to regain the control of the direction of their marriage.

- Charter 5 to 6—These sections help the individual to rediscover oneself and understand his/her past and it's impact in his/ her life and in the marriage.

- Chapter 7 to 9—These chapters lead the individual in self-understanding within the context of the marriage.

- Chapter 10–11—The couple renews their recommitment to their marriage through continuing the process of change.

- Chapter 12—Preventing relapse to old behaviors.

- Chapter 13—Re-evaluating the progress of the strength of their marriage.

This workbook may also serve as a therapist's guide in their working with couples who struggle in understanding the impact of their Family of Origin in relationship.*

Chapter 1—Assessment of the status of my marriage

The focus of Chapter 1 is a "thumbnail" assessment of the issues that lead to the problems and potential breakdown of the marriage. It initiates each partner's self-assessment of their contribution to the potential failure of the relationship.

Chapter 2—Assessment of my marriage skills and its bases

The simple yet difficult recognition that learned behavior is a conditioning that can be unlearned empowers the individuals to take ownership, and to take control of shaping their married life.

For the therapist, this part of the workbook is a fertile ground for working individually with each spouse, helping each toward insight into his and her behavior as-perhaps-reenactment of parent's behavior in their own marriage.

Chapter 3—Communication—How do I sound? What do I mean?

Effective communication between couples happens when both individuals are tuned in to the feeling at the moment, being experienced on the gut level and it is verbalized appropriately. Oftentimes the effect of communication is not based on *what* is said but *how* it is said.

Chapter 4—The accountability I bring to my marriage

This chapter opens up the possibility of restoring hope within the couple for recreating and reconstructing their marriage. Through accountability, the couple is given the opportunity to renew and re-commit themselves to work on their relationship.

Chapter 5—Reacquainting myself with my past experiences through genogram

Working through this chapter is the first step to understanding of one's past, which intends to be the enrichment of the marriage. The Family of Origin's (FOO's) influences can diminish any sense of self and hold a spouse a hostage to earlier experiences. Consequently, the person is unable to define his/her own person.

Chapter 6—Understanding the legacy of the family of origin

The focus is on knowing each individual's own dynamics as generating forth from the legacy of his/her FOO. The influence and confluence of two different backgrounds can be enriching to the couple's life, but oftentimes causes hobbling and crippling conflicts in the relationship. If the FOO's influence has caused the individuals to be fragmented and unsure of themselves, each individual might need therapy individually, especially to identify FOO issues.

Chapter 7—Learning more about me in the context of marriage

It is in the context of relationships that we become aware of the depth of, or the lack of knowledge about ourselves. Who we are is revealed with very particular and concrete details in a very close relationship as in marriage. The dynamics of the couple's relationship will uncover the conditioning they have been oriented to from their FOO, and reveal how their lives have been shaped up to now.

Chapter 8—The uniqueness of each marriage

The uniqueness of each marriage comes from the "baggage" and the "richness" of what each partner brings into the relationship. In taking charge of the health of the marriage, each partner needs to be mindful of their responsibility for its growth without sacrificing their own personal growth.

Chapter 9—The multi-dimensional aspects of marriage

The multi-faceted aspects of our lives continue to present challenges in marriage. Being aware of what they are, being willing to meet and embrace them, has the potential to be the source of strength in unifying the purpose of the joint lives of the couple.

Chapter 10—Moving forward in my marriage

A relationship is never static; there is always an ebb and flow in a marriage. Being able to tune in to this rhythm will allow the couple to develop harmony in their marriage. Any changes that happen within the individuals can cause a certain loss of equilibrium and, subsequently, feelings of insecurity arise. If these dynamics are not understood and accepted, one or both spouses may misconstrue the marriage as breaking up and ending.

Chapter 11—Keeping the commitment alive

Life together as a couple offers challenges that the couple will respond to and adjust to; inevitably, change will be brought about. Partners in the relationship who are not willing to change will soon be feeling that the marriage will fail; and then become convinced of that failure. When this happens the relationship can only continue to worsen unless the couple seeks out and gives themselves to competent and professional help.

Therapy addresses this issue, enhancing each individual's awareness of the growth potential that can be harnessed in the inevitable changes that are bound to occur in the relationship.

Chapter 12—Preventing the return of old behaviors and attitudes

Loving and being loved in marriage is a primeval comfort that makes each individual flourish. However, it takes deliberate intentionality to make a loving commitment, and daily thoughtfulness in maintaining marriage. The essential focus in maintaining marriage can never require the sacrifice of one's individuality. Rather, that focus requires the cultivation of one's gifts as shared gifts with each other. How we manage our individuality will determine our behavior, as our love life determines our attitude.

Each individual's discovery of their own weaknesses and the weaknesses of their spouse within the context of marriage provides opportunity for growth. Mistakes and relapses happen; but this predictable fact is not adequate reason to dissolve the marriage.

Chapter 13—Reevaluating the foundations of the strength of marriage

Recognizing the fact that the process of change does not happen overnight, one has to be honest, steadfast, and confident of achieving equilibrium and harmony in the marriage.

Note: pre-screening and post-screening are conducted to gauge the result of the couples' therapy.

CHAPTER 1

ASSESSMENT OF THE STATUS OF MY MARRIAGE

The success of your marriage is not only finding the right mate but by being the right mate.

—Rabbi Burnett R. Brickner

THERE ARE ESSENTIAL ASPECTS of a healthy marriage. And the elements of a healthy marriage are defined and determined by the couple. These elements may change according to what is demanded of each spouse and their "need" in the different stages of their marriage. The crucial elements that must be maintained are the continuity of trust, loving harmony, and respectful cohesiveness in the couple's relationship. Growth is sustained and promoted in the relationship without stifling the individual, and does not come at the expense of the marriage.

Conversely, the growth of the marriage cannot happen at the expense of each spouse's interest and health.

The absence of basic consideration in the worthiness of a spouse leads to an unhealthy marriage. This negative attitude communicates itself in the way spouse treats each other, and trickles down to the other aspects of the marriage.

Consider carefully the chart on the following page.

In the left column write down the elements of a healthy marriage that are already present in your marriage. Rate yourself and your spouse from 1 (low)—10 (high). In the right column, write down the ones that are not yet present in your marriage but you wish to have.

Compare and contrast your list with your spouse/partner. Decide what is important in both of your lists. Prioritize together the elements you want to work on.

Existing Elements	Self	Spouse	None Existing Elements	Prioritize Your List

Name 5 qualities that attracted you to your spouse when you first met. Are those qualities still present? Yes _____, No_____. If your answer is "no" what now obscures your initial perception?

Name 5 aspirations you have of your marriage, (how you envision your marriage growing?)

Give examples of checks and balances you agreed to have in your marriage: Ex. Agreement that you can't both go "crazy" at the same time. Agree to have a "cooling off time" when getting into a "heated" argument. Agree to maintain boundaries, i.e., respect each other's space.

On a scale of 1 to 10 (high) rate how you perceive yourself and your spouse in the following areas:

	Self	**Spouse**
Trustworthiness	_____	_____
Respectability	_____	_____
Integrity	_____	_____

Assessment of the status of my marriage: *It is highly recommended that, as a couple, you spend 10 to 15 minutes (more time if needed) to share your written responses to the exercises in all parts of the book.*

What brings you to therapy?

_____

_____

_____

_____

_____

_____

_____

_____

_____

_____

_____

_____

_____

Share with each other how you feel about your responses and evaluate what changes you would like to make to improve your rating.

On a scale of 1 to 10 (1= low – 10 = high) how would you rate your marriage? ____

On a scale of 1 to 10 (1= low – 10 = high) how committed are you in making this marriage work? ____

Have you thought of divorce? Yes ___, No ___. If your answer is "yes" what are your thoughts and feelings about it?

_____

_____

_____

_____

_____

_____

_____

_____

_____

_____

_____

_____

_____

_____

_____

_____

_____

_____

_____

Homework:

If you are working with a therapist, demonstrate in the session examples of attempts you have made to communicate with each other effectively in between sessions. Rate from 1 (low) to 10 (high) your satisfaction with your dialogue.

Rate from 1 (low) to 10 (high) basic skills applied in the dialogue:

	Myself	**My Spouse**
1) Engagement in dialogue	_____	_____
2) Effort being put forth in dialogue	_____	_____
3) Listening skill	_____	_____
4) Giving feedback	_____	_____
5) Receiving feedback	_____	_____
6) Openness	_____	_____
7) Willingness to improve dialogue	_____	_____
8) Where you want to be in your ability to dialogue	_____	_____

9) List desired areas of improvement:

Self	**Spouse**
a)	a)
b)	b)
c)	c)
d)	d)
e)	e)

Add more if needed   *Add more if needed*

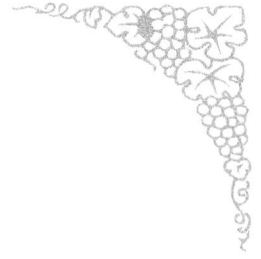

Happiness [is] Only Real When Shared

—Jon Krakauer, Into the Wild

CHAPTER 2

ASSESSMENT OF MARRIAGE SKILLS AND ITS BASES

The greatest happiness in life is the conviction that we are loved—loved for ourselves, or rather, loved in spite of ourselves.

—Victor Hugo

OFTENTIMES THE SKILLS YOU have developed, or the lack of, stem from what you have been exposed to and observed from your parent's interaction. Unwittingly, you internalized and emulated the expressions and behaviors without thought to examining how these affect others, especially your spouse. You might even have thought of these behaviors as "normal," or how things "should be."

Awareness of our skills in relationships comes to the forefront when it is expressed in the context of relationships, particularly in marriage. It is in this context that the core of our being is challenged and oftentimes demands that we re-define our values, reexamine our beliefs and re-discover who we are.

The following questionnaires will help you evaluate your skills that are important in understanding how you were influenced by your family of origin.

Pre-Screening:

Name: _____ Spouse: _____ Date: _____

RELATIONSHIP SKILLS

Rank yourself and your spouse from 1 = low – 10 = high (+) each area of the relationship skills demonstrated in your marriage. Spend 5—10 minutes discussing the differences/ similarities in your rating of each other. Then rate the skills of your father and your mother to gain an understanding of their influence in the development of your own skills.

	Self	Spouse	Father	Mother

Self-management: the ability to deal with stressful situations using the skills below:

	Self	Spouse	Father	Mother
Self-talk (things you think or say to yourself)				
Self-understanding				
Self-care				
Self-esteem				

Relationships: A) The level of comfort and connection made in these different contexts:

	Self	Spouse	Father	Mother
Intra-personal (how you feel/treat yourself)				
Inter-personal (how you feel/treat others)				
Family				
Friends				

Relationships: B) Connection of the couple is operationally expressed in the following areas:

	Self	Spouse	Father	Mother
Intimacy				
Openness				
Expression of feelings				
Emotional engagement (expressed outwardly)				

Feelings: The ability to identify emotions, its source and how it is expressed in action.

	Self	Spouse	Father	Mother
Understanding				
Expressive				
Connecting feeling with behavior				

Communication: Being aware of the effect on others the way one communicates.

Distancing				
Connecting				
Style:				
Assertive				
Aggressive				
Passive				
Passive/Aggressive				

Listening: Being attentive in communication, and in being open in receiving and giving feedback.

Active				
Feedback				
Giving				
Receiving				

DESCRIBE YOUR SELF-EVALUATION ON YOUR RELATIONSHIP SKILLS

What is your dominant rating on the different relationship skills? Which one is the lowest?

_____

_____

_____

_____

_____

What insight did you gain about yourself as a result of this exercise?

_____

_____

_____

_____

_____

Do your self-ratings similar to how you rated your parents? Your father? Your mother? How your spouse rated you?

_____

_____

_____

_____

_____

Based on the scores you gave your parents, what did you see in your parents' relationship that showed strengths and weaknesses in their marriage?

_____

_____

_____

_____

_____

What was it like to reflect on your parents' relationship skills? How does it make you feel about what you have learned about their relationship?

_____

_____

_____

_____

_____

Describe how you perceived their interaction when you were growing-up. How does it compare with your relationship with your spouse?

_____

_____

_____

_____

_____

Name 3 positive and 3 negative traits you have learned or believed to have received from your parents.

	Positive		**Negative**
1)		1)	
2)		2)	
3)		3)	

How are these strengths and weaknesses being played out in your marriage?

_____

_____

_____

_____

If your ratings were mostly 2 or 3s, how does that make you feel? What would you like to do about this?

If you were mostly 7, 8 and 9's what will you do to continue to maintain where you are with your skills?

Write some of your thoughts and feelings about this exercise.

Spend 10 to 15 minutes (more time if needed) to share with your spouse your insights about yourself as a result of working on the area of relationship skills.

_____

_____

_____

_____

_____

_____

_____

_____

_____

_____

_____

_____

_____

_____

_____

_____

Pre-Screening:

Name: _____ Spouse: _____ Date: _____

ELEMENTS OF LOVING RELATIONSHIPS

Rate yourself and your spouse with a "+" or "-" in each area of the elements of loving relationships demonstrated in your marriage. Spend 5 to 10 minutes discussing the differences/similarities in your rating of each other. Then rate your father and your mother to gain an understanding of their influence in establishing the elements in your own marriage. Put a question mark if you are unsure.

The Elements	Self	Spouse	Father	Mother
Commitment—values the permanency of the relationship.				
Promises exclusivity				
Sees good in the relationship				
Values the investment in the relationship				
Aware of part in the problem				
Intimacy—values emotional closeness				
Sees good in self and spouse				
Affirms the value of the other person				
Appreciates the other person's action				
Affection is shown verbally and physically				
Caring—shows concern for another's welfare				
Trustworthy				
Reliable				
Protective—maintains integrity as a couple				
Spends meaningful time as a couple				
Enjoyment—as individuals & as a couple				
Negotiates activities that are pleasurable				
Initiates enjoyable activities				
Responsibility—accepts share of problems				

Accepts interdependence in the relationship				
Does not blame others				
Sharing hurt—in order to find a solution				
Recognizes that anger masks other feelings				
Looks at pattern of hurtful behavior				
Examines the source of hurtful behavior				
Forgiveness—acceptance and understanding				
Validates hurt in self and partner				
Recognizes that unforgiven hurts = resentment				
Passion—affection, longing, sexual intimacy				
Shares likes and dislikes				
Spontaneous				
Inner harmony				

REFLECTION ON THE ELEMENTS OF LOVING RELATIONSHIPS

Do the pluses and minuses for your parents confirmed what you thought/perceived of their relationship?

_____

_____

_____

_____

_____

_____

What do you recognize as strong elements of the loving relationship in your parent's marriage?

_____

_____

_____

_____

_____

_____

Do the pluses and minuses you marked for your parents reflect what you thought of their relationship when you were growing-up? Describe.

_____

_____

_____

_____

_____

Describe your perception of your own and your spouse's pluses and minuses marks. Are they where you want them to be? Do the marks replicate your parent's marks?

_____

_____

_____

_____

_____

How does identifying the important elements in your relationship helpful in enhancing your marriage.

_____

_____

_____

_____

_____

_____

Compare with your spouse what you both identified as important elements in your relationship.

_____

_____

_____

_____

_____

Prioritize as to WHAT ELEMENTS IN YOUR RELATIONSHIP you can agree to work on to strengthen your marriage?

_____

_____

_____

_____

_____

_____

Spend 10 to 15 minutes (more time if needed) to share with your spouse your insights about yourself as a result of working on the Elements of a loving relationship.

_____

_____

_____

_____

_____

_____

_____

_____

_____

_____

_____

Re-assess your progress in your communication. Rank each area on a scale of 1 to 10: 1 = low – 10 = high your satisfaction with your dialogue _____. If you perceived that you have not made progress, talked about what hinders your ability to move forward in this area. Rate from 1 (low) to 10 (high) basic skills applied in the dialogue.

	Myself	**My Spouse**
1) Engagement in dialogue	_____	_____
2) Effort being put forth in dialogue	_____	_____
3) Listening skill	_____	_____
4) Giving feedback	_____	_____
5) Receiving feedback	_____	_____
6) Openness	_____	_____
7) Willingness to improve dialogue	_____	_____
8) Where you want to be in your ability to dialogue	_____	_____

9) List desired areas of improvement:

Self	**Spouse**
a)	a)
b)	b)
c)	c)
d)	d)
e)	e)

Add more if needed　　　　　　　*Add more if needed*

CHAPTER 3

COMMUNICATION: HOW DO I SOUND? WHAT DO I MEAN?

The intrinsic value of communication depends on how you make each other feel, in silence and in speaking. Non-verbal communication often delivers a message louder and clearer than the expressed words.

WEBSTER DICTIONARY DEFINES THE word "communicate" (communication) to mean: speech, talk, intercourse, expression, contact or conversation.

Effective communication between couples happens when the individual is tuned into the feeling being experienced on a gut level, and verbalized appropriately. Oftentimes the effect of communication is not based on what is said but how it is said. Communication is essential in the person's growth and development because:

- It is the only vehicle in which we can address problems.
- It is a means in understanding yourself and others.
- It is an instrument in understanding problems particularly in relationships.
- It is the only vehicle in facilitating growth in relationships

Husbands and wives do not always need words to communicate. Communication can be by touching, eye contact, and attitude.

Five examples of your spouse's indirect manner of communication	Your perception of its underlying meaning

GUIDELINES FOR EFFECTIVE COMMUNICATION

Understanding the differences between men's and women's emotional make up is a way of developing empathy and narrowing the gap in communication between genders.

If you are the "emotional type," check your emotion, and identify the underlying basis for it before you speak or respond. If you have the tendency to respond "intellectually" focus on how you feel and how your partner might be feeling at the moment in order to speak/respond with empathy.

Consider these guidelines for any communications between you and your spouse:

1) State your concern to your spouse: ONE ISSUE AT A TIME. Do not bring up past issues.

2) Take ownership of what is happening with you when communicating, when sharing or when presenting a problem. Use *"I" statements*. The sequence of the *thought, feeling*, and *behavior* can be expressed interchangeably.

- Thoughts you want to share with your spouse
- Feelings associated with the thought
- Behavior related to the feelings and thoughts

3) In responding to your spouse:

- *Share* understanding of what was said.
- *Share* your thoughts about what was said.
- *Share* your feelings about what was said.
- *Share* how what was said affects your behavior.

Note well: In any response be open to exploring your reactions to the information communicated to you…use reflective listening…clarify and check out your own assumptions…or, clarify and check out what you think you heard.

Making assumptions is the precursor to the breakdown of communication.

Examples of assumptions:

- you know the meaning of the other person's words.
- you know how the other person feels at this moment.
- you can interpret the other person's facial expressions, behaviors, gestures.

If you think your assumption is correct, avoid making conclusive remark. Check it out by asking if the other person is upset, angry, troubled, sad, etc. Your asking will come across as an attempt to be understanding and/ or empathetic.

4) **Come to a conclusion about the issues.** If you cannot agree, be willing to revisit the issue and consider compromising after giving it some thought. Do not get in the state of mind of "winning or losing" the argument. Remember compromising toward the conclusion of any issue is important in the growth of your marriage. Effective communication results in a win-win situation.

5) **Set another time to talk about it.**

Examples:

6) I have been thinking about my feeling distant or my feeling disconnected from you. As you probably have noticed I have been avoiding any confrontation because don't want to argue anymore.

7) When you talk down to me I feel hurt and it makes me feel like a child. I don't like to be subjected to this; so I avoid bringing up anything at all with you. But I don't like it when we are not speaking with each other.

Self-monitoring and self-management with plan of action

Be aware of bodily signals triggered by situations.

- Tension reduction—deep breathing
  Count 1, 2, 3 clear your mind by picturing the numbers as you take deep breaths through your nose. Hold it for a second, and breathe out through your mouth counting in your head 3, 2, 1 as you feel the tension in your body being released.

- Deliberation of action—understanding the source of action
  Reacting: action is based on the past, displaced focus
  Responding: action is focused on the here and now

- Application
  Reframing your perception: looking at the situation differently, not tunnel vision.

Cognitive restructuring: changing negative self- talk to positive self-talk.

Now practice, practice, practice and practice some more. On-going communication in marriage is very important because as the years go by the couples will experience changes in their behavior, goals, desires and needs.

COUPLE'S THERAPY AGREEMENT WITH AN UNDERSTANDING AND ACCEPTANCE OF THE FOLLOWING PREMISES:

- I am participating in this couple therapy accepting that my marriage is a partnership, and I have an equal role in the relationship. What I have to say is as important as what my partner has to say.

- I am willing to work on my personal growth unselfishly, understanding that my growth will contribute to the growth of the relationship.

- I will show respect and trust by maintaining confidentiality.

- I will be open to the best of my ability:
    - By sharing about myself
        - By responding to feedback without hostility either verbal or physical

- I will refrain from making any decision about my marriage until I have completed this program.

- I will respect the ground rules established for this couple therapy, and I am willing to contribute by making positive suggestion about the existing rules.

_____   _____
Signature of one spouse   Witness (Other spouse)

_____   _____
Date   Date

"Coming together is a beginning;
keeping together is progress;
working together is success."

—Henry Ford

CHAPTER 4

THE ACCOUNTABILITY I BRING TO MY MARRIAGE

...perhaps the central paradox of our condition—that what we hunger for perhaps more than anything else is to be known in our full humanness, and yet that is often just what we also fear more than anything else. It is important to tell at least from time to time the secret of who we truly and fully are even if we tell it only to ourselves—because otherwise we run the risk of losing track of who we truly and fully are and little by little come to accept instead the highly edited version which we put forth in hope that the world will find it more acceptable than the real thing.

—Frederick Buechner–Telling Secrets

ACCOUNTABILITY IMPLIES BEING RESPONSIBLE for one's action. The first step requires the individual's self-awareness, self-understanding and openness through self-reflection. Willingness to be accountable in relationships brings about a firmer conviction to be the best person in an important relationship—your marriage.

This would require flexibility and adaptability to benefit you as an individual and the relationship.

It is our own individual responsibility to understand our feelings and behaviors that would affect others, most especially our spouse.

1—I HAVE TO KNOW ME

Before I can understand and solve a problem (or problems) in my marriage, I need to understand myself first. _____ Agree _____ Disagree. Why?

_____

_____

_____

2—I AM THE ONLY ONE WHO CAN CHANGE ME

I can start with small things I can change about me that will make a big difference in my relationship with my spouse. _____ Agree _____ Disagree.

Example: _____

Explain?

_____

_____

_____

3—I, ONLY, AM RESPONSIBLE FOR MY FEELINGS

I take responsibility for how I react/respond to my spouse's behavior/ communication and what I do with it. _____ Agree _____ Disagree

Explain?

_____

_____

_____

Based on the questionnaires you have completed, on a scale of 1 (low) to 10(high) how willing are you to go through the processes as described below:

_____   The process of uncovering the profound issues interfering with my growth and, therefore, with the growth of my marriage.

_____   The process of painfully learning honesty and determination are needed to admit my problems.

_____   The process of hurtfully stumbling across the ancient fact that it is my prerogative to change or not to change.

_____   The process of discovering that the growth of my marriage depends on partnership, that neither my spouse nor myself can do it alone.

Circle Y = Yes, N = No to demonstrate your willingness to work on the following premises:

- If personal issues are not addressed prior or parallel with couple's work, achieving any change in the relationship is unlikely. Y   N

- Each one has the responsibility to make a choice to live (or not), in the "status quo" of the relationship. Note well: In certain instances the choice may inevitably result in the termination of the marriage. Y   N

- It is the responsibility of each individual to seek help if personal issues interfere in each partner's personal growth and in the growth of the marriage. Y   N

Making the commitment to complete this manual is projected as being a personal reward:

- Rediscovery of oneself in the intimacy of the most important person in your life, your spouse.

- Deeply felt and fully appreciated personal growth and concomitant with the growth of your marriage.

Spend 10 to 15 minutes (more time if needed) to share with your spouse your insights about yourself as a result of working on the above exercises.

_____

_____

_____

_____

_____

From all of your arguments and fights (past and present) make a list of YOUR OWN hurtful or unacceptable behaviors YOU ACTED-OUT toward your spouse. On a scale of 1 (low) to 10 (high), rate each behavior as to how difficult it would be for you to change that behavior.

And then, using the same scale, rate your level of commitment to change that behavior on the following chart.

<u>Level of Change</u>

Behaviors	Difficulty	Commitment

If you were married to a person like yourself, what changes would you like that person to make?

_____

_____

_____

_____

_____

If the person is not aware of the changes he /she needs to make, what would be the best way to help that person to be aware of the changes he/she needs to make?

_____

_____

_____

_____

_____

Spend 10 to 15 minutes (more time if needed) to share with each other your written responses to the exercises.

_____

_____

_____

_____

_____

Pre-Screening:

Name: _____ Spouse _____Date: _____

THE FRAMEWORK OF YOUR BEHAVIOR IN RELATIONSHIP

Rank yourself and your spouse from 1 = low – 10 = high (+) each area of the framework of your behavior demonstrated in your marriage. Spend 5 to 10 minutes discussing the differences/similarities in your rating of each other.

Then rate the traits of your father and your mother to gain an understanding of their influence in the development of your own traits.

	Self	Spouse	Father	Mother

Responsibility—the couple functions as equal partners. Imbalanced shows in either action below:

Enabling				
Controlling				
Over-responsible				
Under-responsible				

Reality Orientation—the ability to stay in the "here and now" to assess situations.

Impulsivity				
Compulsivity				
Isolation				
Shame				
Guilt				

Escapism—Inability to remain grounded in reality to focus on what is of value in the relationship.

Substance abuse				
Workaholism				
Gambling				
Sex—pornography, infidelity (specify)				
Computer activity				
Other (specify)				

Abuse— Misuse of power that degrades the other person.

Physical				
Verbal				
Emotional				
Sexual				

DESCRIBE YOUR RESPONSES IN THE EXERCISE ON THE FRAMEWORK OF YOUR BEHAVIOR IN A RELATIONSHIP:

What was it like to reflect on how you perceived your own (spouse, parents) framework of relationship?

_____

_____

_____

_____

_____

How strong was the framework of your (spouse, parents) relationship? What aspects of the framework were lacking? Which were present?

_____

_____

_____

_____

In doing this exercise, did you discover that you might be re-enacting in your own marriage the same problems you have seen in your parent's marriage because of undefined framework of relationship?

_____

_____

_____

_____

What on-going stress did you observed your parents had to deal with? What effect did the stress had on them?

_____

_____

_____

_____

_____

What did you learn from seeing how your parents deal with stress?

_____

_____

_____

_____

_____

How is your way of dealing with stress affect your marriage?

_____

_____

_____

_____

_____

Did you gain new awareness in regard to your relationship to your spouse and parents?

_____

_____

_____

_____

_____

Have you developed some understanding of yourself?

_____

_____

_____

_____

_____

Spend 10 to 15 minutes (more time if needed) to share with your spouse your insights about yourself as a result of working on the Framework of your Behavior in Relationship.

_____

_____

_____

_____

_____

_____

_____

_____

_____

_____

_____

_____

_____

_____

TOOL BOX:
TO REPAIR AND ENRICH MY MARRIAGE

In the first column list the things (skills) you would like to have in your tool box. In the second column rate yourself 1 to 5 (1 being low, 5 being high) for each tool you have on your list. In the third column write the number where you would like to be. Then do all this again for your spouse. What do you want your spouse to have in his/her toolbox!

Me	Now	Goal	My Spouse	Now	Goal

Be specific how you are going to get hold of these tools you want; and how to make your own changes to get to where you would like to be.

Tools	Specific ways of getting hold of these tools

What is your compelling reason to change? How do you identify the need for change?

| |
| |
| |
| |
| |
| |
| |
| |
| |

Spend 10 to 15 minutes (more time if needed) to share with each other your written responses to the exercises. Put reflection below.

_____

_____

_____

_____

_____

_____

_____

<u>Re-assess your progress in your communication.</u>

Rate from 1 (low) to 10 (high) your satisfaction with your dialogue _____

Rate from 1 (low) to 10 (high) basic skills applied in the dialogue: _____

	Myself	**My Spouse**
1) Engagement in dialogue	_____	_____
2) Effort being put forth in dialogue	_____	_____
3) Listening skill	_____	_____
4) Giving feedback	_____	_____
5) Receiving feedback	_____	_____
6) Openness	_____	_____
7) Willingness to improve dialogue	_____	_____
8) Where you want to be in your ability to dialogue	_____	_____

9) List desired areas of improvement:

Self	**Spouse**
a)	a)
b)	b)
c)	c)
d)	d)
e)	e)

Add more if needed   *Add more if needed*

Generation—Family—Love

Wisdom—Loyalty—Strengh

Experience—Harmony—Hope

Understanding—Support

Roots—Honesty—Being

Partnertship—Fun

Forgiveness

Comfort

Issues

Self

Role

Peace

Meaning

Faithfulness

CHAPTER 5

REACQUAINTING MYSELF WITH MY PAST EXPERIENCES THROUGH THE GENOGRAM

When you teach your son, you teach your son's son.

—The Talmud

THE GENOGRAM/GENEALOGY IS A great way of mapping out our family tree. It allows us to trace multigenerational characteristics, conditionings, predispositions and family traits. The goal is not to blame but to take responsibility for our behavior and to initiate changes within ourselves that will ultimately enrich our marriage. The work is toward:

- ✓ Being aware of the healthy and the unhealthy learned behaviors from parents and grandparents.

- ✓ Consciously understanding our emotional inheritance from parents and grandparents.

- ✓ Realizing the length, breadth and depth of our own uniqueness.

Directions in completing the genogram

Use the diagram, Fig. A, to work on your genogram. You can fill in/expand your genogram based on how extensive the members of your family.

The symbols and meanings, Fig.B and Fig. C, will help you map out the connection you have with your immediate family and multi-generational family members. As you answer the guideline questions, reflect on what you "know" or have heard about the habits, traits, behaviorism (+/-), and medical and mental predispositions of members of your family; parents, grandparents and great grandparents, uncles, aunts and cousins. A pattern will emerge that will help you understand the "picture"/self-perception you have about yourself. This will also help you in understanding how you have "become you."

Refer to pages 45, 46, 47, 48 and 49, work on the exercise to get a sense of your experience as a young person. "How did I become ME?" on pages 51, 52, 53, 54, 55 and 56 will help you to look at the legacy you have been handed down by your family members who came before you. Finally, work on page 49. Identify the legacy you received from your Family of Origin, then make a decision formulating the legacy you would like to leave your children. Identify what legacy you hope your children will pass on to their children.

Problems in the developmental process of a child/adolescent result in fragmentation of the self. The ability to become a whole person is compromised. Becoming a unique individual (forming an IDENTITY) fails from the lack of validation by the most important people in a young life—the parents. All future relationships suffer the consequences.

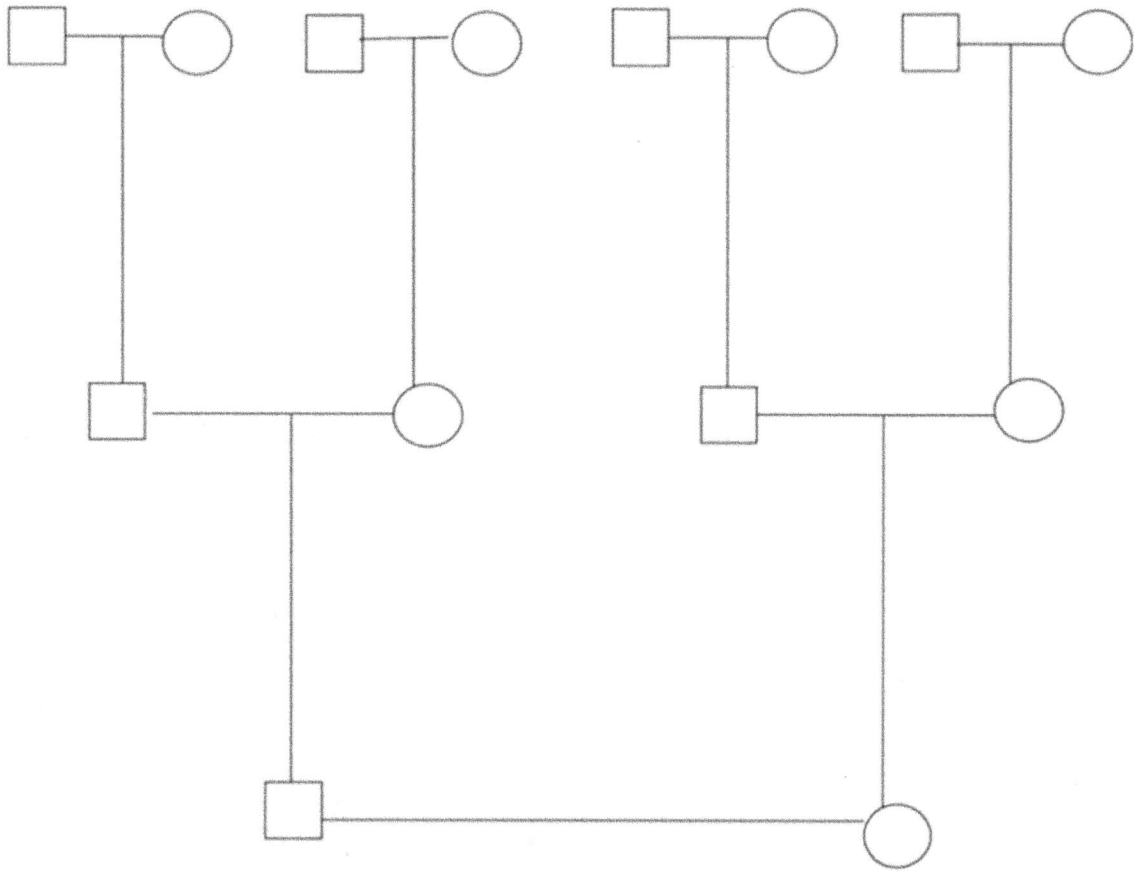

GENOGRAM
Fig. A

GENOGRAM: SYMBOLS AND MEANINGS

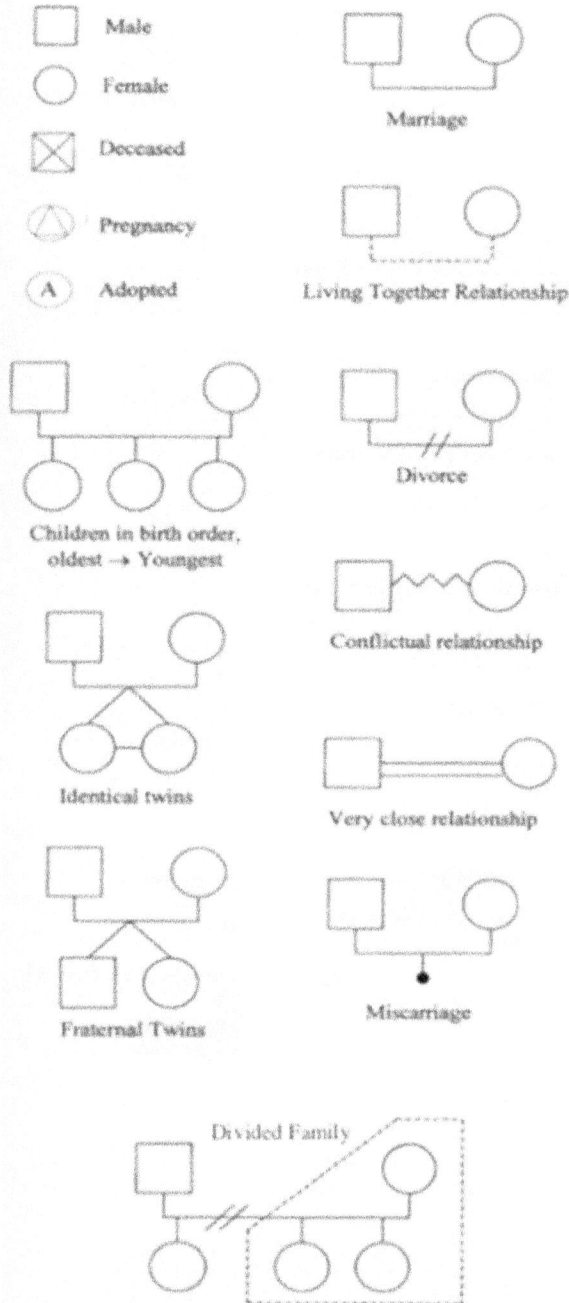

Male

Female

Deceased

Pregnancy

A   Adopted

Marriage

Living Together Relationship

Divorce

Children in birth order,
oldest → Youngest

Conflictual relationship

Identical twins

Very close relationship

Fraternal Twins

Miscarriage

Divided Family

Conflicted Relationship
Parties involved do not get along
There is tension in the relationship.

Close Relationship
Healthy relationship – people involved are
caring and supportive of each other.

Very close relationship
Over involved – unhealthy relationship
characterized by being very dependent on each other.

Distant Relationship
Lack of involvement between two people,
and avoidance of each other

● ● ●

Cutoff Relationship
Two parties are estranged from each other due to
unresolved negative emotional attachment.
No contact but strong negative tie remains

Fig. B   Fig. C

Adapted from the book Genograms by Emily Marlin

Family-of-Origin brief self-assessment tools

Factors enabling me to succeed in my self-enhancement process, and in my marriage.

1) Attitude toward couple's work: Circle the one which applies to you.

    • Reality based self-determination—willingness to work through issues from my past which impact my life, and to understand my strengths and weaknesses that influence my current behavior, thinking and feeling.

    • Instinctively based self-determination—planning my life the way I am now, without having to look back into my past.

2) Rate yourself from 1 – 10 = being more willing to engage in the couple's therapy:

	Where I am now	Where I want to be
Openness	_____	_____
Honesty	_____	_____
Motivation	_____	_____
Self-disclosure	_____	_____
Self-exploration	_____	_____
Willingness to change	_____	_____

Guidelines in working your genogram. Please respond to the following questions:

As a child

☐ Did my parents fulfill or meet my needs?

☐ Did my parents make me feel "OK" or good about myself?

☐ Did I feel safe?

☐ Was I encouraged to express my thoughts and feelings?

☐ Did I have someone who believed in me, and/or listened to me or both?

☐ Was my family nurturing, trusting and validating?

☐ Did I learn to love, to trust, to listen and to share?

☐ What behaviors did I see in my family that made me feel uncomfortable?

☐ What thoughts do I have about these behaviors?

Check the following early life issues that you experienced and need to work on with yourself:

Early life issues

_____ Abuse: physical, sexual, emotional, inappropriate age-related responsibilities

_____ Medical illness: family member, myself

_____ Family substance abuse problems

_____ Family mental health problems: depression, obsessive compulsive disorder, suicide attempts, etc.

_____ Divorce, death, poor parenting

_____ Abandonment issues, physical, emotional neglect

_____ Poor family interrelationship

        _____ Lack of communication

        _____ Poor interaction

        _____ Not feeling safe

        Others:

Formative years

_____ Problems in school socially and academically

_____ Truancy and absenteeism

_____ Involvement in alcohol and drug use in teen years

        Others:

Experiences as a young person

Check and circle what is applicable. If you experienced the opposite of what is listed below, write it down.

- Losses: divorce death separation moving
- Neglect
- Coldness
- Overprotection
- Hostility
- Intrusiveness
- Absent/ emotionally distant parent

- Over/under stimulation
- Inconsistent/insufficient control
- Abuse: physical emotional sexual
- Mental illness
- Medical illness
- Obsessive/ compulsive behaviors: over cleanliness alcoholism workaholism food
- Family financial difficulties
- Other (specify or explain)

Spend 10 to 15 minutes (more time if needed) to share with your spouse your insights about yourself as a result of working on your genogram.

_____

_____

_____

_____

_____

_____

_____

_____

Positive experiences give us strengths to meet the challenges in life and relationships. Describe the memorable experience(s) that make you who you are today.

_____

_____

_____

_____

_____

_____

_____

_____

CHAPTER 6

UNDERSTANDING THE LEGACY OF THE FAMILY OF ORIGIN

You can kiss your family and friends good-bye and put miles between you, but at the same time you carry them with you in your heart your mind, your stomach, because you do not just live in a world but a world lives in you.

—*Frederick Buechner, Telling the Truth*

UNDERSTANDING OUR DEVELOPMENTAL PROCESS will help us to become more aware of our deficits, faults and strengths. It is in the early stages of development that we learn the how-to's in relationships: how to love, how to express feelings, how identify our needs and take charge of our responsibilities as we had learned at an early age grounded in age appropriate developmental tasks. *Deficits in the developmental process result in the perception that relationships are not safe.*

HOW DID I BECOME ME?

It is difficult to admit to ourselves the truth about the extent to which our parents may have influenced or hurt us as children. There are some of us who experienced early trauma in life that were painful and shameful. To protect ourselves from the pain we learned to build defenses. One of these is to shut down, or numb our feelings. We develop "amnesia" for our feelings. If later in life, the feeling is triggered, we "forget" the origin.

Negative experiences during a person's development *malinger* on his/her life:

o Through a generic sense of mistrust in close relationships

_____

_____

_____

_____

_____

o   Through ignoring the needs of the self when adapting to survive in any environment of rigid roles and rules

_____

_____

_____

_____

_____

o   Through the failure to take possession of the innate talents he/she is given

_____

_____

_____

_____

_____

In order to survive in an environment of rigid rules and roles, we adjust who we are and ignore our needs. The consequence is failure to develop the person we are meant to be.

HOW WELL DO I KNOW MYSELF?—Respond to the following:

➢   What pain, shame, trauma, etc., have I experienced that resulted in destructive, dysfunctional or self-defeating behaviors?

_____

_____

_____

_____

_____

➢   What incidents or people helped bring about my self-awareness?

_____

_____

_____

_____

_____

➢   What are my behaviors that resulted in my distancing rather than connecting in my relationships with others

_____

_____

_____

_____

_____

➤ What feedback do I get about myself from important individuals in my life

_____

_____

_____

_____

_____

IDENTIFY AND CHECK THE DEFICITS YOU FIND WITHIN YOURSELF

☐ Inability to identify feelings/needs

☐ Inability to trust others

☐ Over controlling

☐ Lack of control

☐ Overly responsible

☐ No sense of responsibility

☐ Rigid boundaries

☐ Lacking boundaries

☐ Distorted self-image

☐ Anger

☐ Defensiveness

Positive traits gained from your early experiences. Check the assets that apply:

	To you	To your spouse
☐ Empathy	_____	_____
☐ Understanding	_____	_____
☐ Tolerance	_____	_____
☐ Attentiveness	_____	_____
☐ Patience	_____	_____
☐ Perseverance	_____	_____
☐ Openness	_____	_____
☐ Kindness	_____	_____
☐ Humor	_____	_____
☐ Motivation	_____	_____
☐ Determination	_____	_____

☐ Inner Harmony   _____   _____

☐ Inner Strength   _____   _____

☐ Acceptance   _____   _____

☐ Others (Identify)   _____   _____

THE INFLUENCE OF MY *FAMILY OF ORIGIN*

- The family of origin affects three generations, at least.

_____

- All family dynamics are based on multigenerational legacy.

_____

The strengths you have inherited from your parents, you may choose to cultivate. The limitations that you identify in yourself, even though it might be rooted from many generations before you, it can be changed to break the cycle of undesirable traits. You have the chance to choose to be the best person you can be as an individual and in your marriage. The knowledge you gain from the process will help in defining the legacy you choose to pass on to your own children.

What we learned from our parents is what learned from their own parents. We are operating based on the legacy of their parents, their parent's parents, etc. We have to consider what legacy we would like to hand down to our children. Are you "OK" with what you learned from your parents?

DESCRIBE YOUR RELATIONSHIP AND THE LEGACY PASSED ON WITH EACH GENERATION:

- YOUR FAMILY OF ORIGIN

- YOUR PRESENT NUCLEAR FAMILY

- YOUR CHILDREN'S GENERATION

WHO AM I?

Write notes to yourself of your insights, feelings and thoughts about your insights.

Share key points with your spouse.

Hold an open dialogue with your spouse about your findings.

<u>Continue to write what you think and feel is needed</u>

To explore the roots of your marriage you must go back to your family of origin—not to blame your parents but to develop an understanding of what is behind the dynamics of your marriage. Without awareness and acceptance of the losses you have experienced, healing and becoming an integrated person is not possible.

Based on the questionnaires you have completed, on a scale of 1 (low) to 10 (high) how willing are you to go through the processes as described below:

_____   The process of uncovering the profound issues interfering with my growth and therefore with the growth of my marriage.

_____   The process of painfully learning honesty and determination are needed to admit my problems.

_____   The process of hurtfully stumbling across the ancient fact that *it is my prerogative to change or not to change.*

_____   The process of discovering that the growth of my marriage depends on partnership, that neither my spouse nor myself can do it alone.

"The greatest favor we can do our children is to give visible example of love and esteem to our spouse. As they grow up, they may then look forward to maturity so they too can find such love."

—Eucharista War

CHAPTER 7

LEARNING MORE ABOUT ME IN THE CONTEXT OF MY MARRIAGE

A good relationship has a pattern like a dance, and is built on some of the same rules. The partners do not need to hold on tightly, because they move confidently in the same pattern, intricate but gay and swift and free, like a country dance of Mozart's. To touch heavily would be to arrest the pattern and freeze the movement, to check the endlessly changing beauty of its unfolding. There is no place here for the possessive clutch, the clinging arm, the heavy hand, only the barest touch is assigned. Now arm in arm, now face to face, now back to back—it does not matter which. Because they know they are partners moving to the same rhythm, creating a pattern together, and being invisibly nourished by it. The joy of such pattern is not only the joy of creation or the joy of participation; it is also the joy living in the moment. Lightness of touch and living in the moment are intertwined.

When you love someone, you do not love them all the time, in exactly the same way, from moment to moment. It is impossibility. It is even a lie to pretend to. And yet this is exactly what most of us demand. We have so little faith in the ebb and flow of life, of love, of relationships. We leap at the flow of the tide and resist in terror its ebb. We are afraid it will never return. We insist on permanency, on duration, on continuity, when the only continuity possible, in life as in love, as in growth, in fluidity–in freedom, in the sense that the dancers are free, barely touching as they pass, but partners in the same pattern.

The only security is not owning or possessing, not in demanding or expecting, not in hoping even. Security in a relationship lies neither in looking back to what was in nostalgia, nor forward to what it might be in dread or anticipation, but living in the present relationship and accepting it as it is now. Relationships must be like islands, one must accept them for what they are, here and now, within their limits—Islands, surrounded and interrupted by the sea, and continually visited and abandoned by the tides.

—Anne Morrow Lindbergh

Gift From The Sea (1906—2001)

The basic problems in most marriages stem not from the family of origin issues. It is because we failed to trust ourselves to accept who we are, who we can be.

As adults we might be cognitively aware
of the changes we need to make to
sustain a mature, nurturing
relationship. However, the
fragmentation of our
childhood makes it
difficult to share
what we are
not sure we
have…
namely,
OURSELVES.
We look to our
spouse to fill the needs
we missed in our childhood,
unaware that our spouse is
possibly in the same boat as we are.

Communication is barren and unproductive without openness. *The opportunities to be known by each other are constrained without honesty and intimacy.*

THE EXPERIENCE OF SELF-VALIDATION from your family of origin often times correlate with your level of self-acceptance and self-confidence. This personal experience influences how open you are and your ability to entrust your inner-most being to another person, believing that it will be honored. Consequently, you are predisposed to a certain level of intimacy. This level of intimacy means communicating one's positive and negative aspects and being accepted by each other.

Acceptance

I accept who you are, but I will not accept behaviors that disrespect me. I value who I am. I would like to foster these good feelings of who I am. I'm not perfect. Through acceptance my faults shall be the stepping stones that will help me to grow if they are pointed out to me with kindness.

Circle what apply to you that prevent you from being able to communicate openly and effectively with your spouse:

- Avoidance of feeling vulnerable
- Lack of communication skills
- Unaware of what to share
- Lack of insight about oneself
- Inability to trust
- Inability to change poor habits in communicating
- Fear of change
- Fear of not being accepted

Allow yourself to be vulnerable by sharing with your spouse what you have identified as your reason(s) for your difficulty in communicating openly. Spend as much time as you need to create an atmosphere of trust and respect at this time of taking the risk of being open.

SELF-DISCOVERY IN MARRIAGE... is willingness to take the risk of being intimately known by your spouse.

- Five ways of demonstrating how open I am, or how willing I am to entrust my inner most being to my spouse.

- What are the positive and/or negative aspects about me that I can share, believing that it will be accepted by my spouse?

POSITIVE	NEGATIVE

My expectations in my marriage that have its origin in what I learned from my family of origin? Differentiate negative and positive expectations.

POSITIVE	NEGATIVE

Spend 10 to 15 minutes (more time if needed) to share with your spouse your insights about yourself as a result of working on the Framework of relationship.

_____

_____

_____

_____

_____

_____

Expectations are resentments waiting to happen.

What are my expectations in my marriage?	How can I prevent my expectations from turning into resentments?

....since most of our hurts come through relationships so will our healing.

WM Paul Young—The Shack

When we experience conflict in our marriage, we must learn to make an assessment: Is it reality based, or, is it rooted in the family of origin? Write what this means to you?

Spend 10 to 15 minutes (more time if needed) to share with each other your written responses to the exercises.

_____

_____

_____

_____

_____

_____

_____

_____

TAKE YOUR MARRIAGE PULSE

Through understanding your relationship with your parents as an adult.

You are a product of your family of origin, conditioned to think, feel and respond in a specific way. *Oftentimes your relationships with your parents are reflected or re-enacted in your relationship with our spouse.*

1) It is difficult to establish boundary between myself and my family of origin (include siblings). Circle one: [Agree–Disagree] Write your comment:

_____

_____

_____

_____

_____

2) My parents do not recognize me as an adult. Circle one: [Agree–Disagree] Write your comment:

_____

_____

_____

_____

_____

3) I am not able to hold my own, or feel like an adult when I am with my parents. Circle one: [Agree–Disagree] Write your comment:

_____

_____

_____

_____

_____

4) I avoid long visits with my parents. Circle one: [Agree–Disagree] Write your comment:

_____

_____

_____

_____

_____

5) I do not feel comfortable accepting gifts from my parents. Circle one: [Agree–Disagree] Write your comment:

_____

_____

_____

_____

_____

6) My parent's gifts, monetary or otherwise, come with 'strings attached."Circle one: [Agree–Disagree] Write your comment:

_____

_____

_____

_____

_____

7) The opinions of my parents influence my major decisions. Circle one: [Agree–Disagree] Write your comment:

_____

_____

_____

_____

_____

8) I shut down to avoid conflict with my parents. Circle one: [Agree–Disagree] Write your comment:

_____

_____

_____

_____

_____

9) I have strong emotional reactions when I hear myself sounding like my mother / father. Circle one: [Agree–Disagree] Write your comment:

_____

_____

_____

_____

_____

10) I have strong reactions to criticism from my parents. Circle one: [Agree–Disagree] Write your comment:

_____

_____

_____

_____

_____

11) My parent's negative remarks outweigh their positive ones. Circle one: [Agree–Disagree] Write your comment:

_____

_____

_____

_____

_____

12) My parents have an impact on my style of handling conflicts with my spouse. Circle one: [Agree–Disagree] Write your comment:

_____

_____

_____

_____

_____

13) I purposely try to be different from my parents. Circle one: [Agree–Disagree] Write your comment:

_____

_____

_____

_____

_____

14) My parents control me (or will control me) even from the grave! Circle one: [Agree–Disagree] Write your comment:

_____

_____

_____

_____

_____

- I wish to change (some, most, all) of the above. Circle one: [Agree–Disagree]

_____

_____

_____

- Identify and explain which statement(s) has impacted you most.

_____

_____

_____

- Describe the impact of what you have learned from this exercise in regard to your relationship with your parents.

_____

_____

_____

- How is it reflected in your relationship with your spouse?

_____

_____

_____

Spend 10 to 15 minutes (more time if needed) to share with each other your written responses to the exercises.

_____

_____

_____

_____

_____

_____

_____

_____

_____

_____

_____

_____

_____

_____

CHAPTER 8

THE UNIQUENESS OF EACH MARRIAGE

More marriages might survive if the partners realized that sometimes the better comes after the worse.

—Doug Larson

WE BRING TO OUR marriage what we have learned from our family of origin, and with it, "built-in" lessons, we bring in certain expectations. Consequently, the uniqueness of the marriage is predicated on what was.

The past experiences may result in the perception that relationships are safe or not safe.

We become aware, or have a hint of the pain we unconsciously buried as a child, when we are reminded of the negative experiences in close relationships as adults. This is particularly true in marriage. Often, when problems begin to surface, couples deal with it in a destructive way. Unknowingly, they sabotage the opportunity to develop a close relationship with their responses in the areas of relationship, responsibilities and in their inability to be grounded in the reality of the "here and now." The uniqueness of the marriage is shaped by what we bring to it.

Even though an age-old tree has been through many storms of life it is still standing. This resembles marriages that weathered the ebb and flow of life, which defined its foundation and strength. (Bishop D. Downing, Author)

Taking charge of the health of your marriage

o   Describe your marriage.

_____

_____

_____

_____

_____

A static marriage is not healthy.

o   Describe what signs you might see if your marriage is stagnant.

_____

_____

_____

_____

_____

A marriage in crisis can be healthy one.

Describe how the statements below apply to your marriage.

o   As a couple, I am not content with the status quo of my relationship.

_____

_____

_____

_____

_____

o   Changes are required to heal my marriage.

_____

_____

_____

_____

_____

o   Each partner plays a vital role in making the changes. The efforts of one person alone cannot improve a marriage. My responsibilities in improving my marriage are:

_____

_____

_____

_____

_____

Spend 10 to 15 minutes (more time if needed) to share with each other your written responses to the exercises.

_____

_____

_____

_____

_____

_____

_____

_____

_____

_____

Describe the uniqueness of your marriage. Write notes of your insights, feelings, and thoughts about it.

<u>Continue to write your feeling and what you think is needed to change and share it with your spouse</u>

_____

_____

_____

_____

_____

_____

_____

_____

_____

THE 3R'S OF MARRIAGE ISSUE THEMES

1) **Reality-Based Orientation**—is being grounded on the "here and now" as the frame of reference in responding to current events particularly in situations related to marriage. Are you in tune with the present?

Inability to focus on the present may be an indicator of the influence of the family of origin, consequently responses to present situation may not be reality-based.

Identify (by checking indicators) your behaviors and your spouse's when reality based thinking is lacking:

	Myself	My Spouse
Impulsive		
Feeling shame		
Feeling guilt		
Isolation		
Poor self-worth image		
Escapism—addiction, gambling, compulsivity		
Abusive—physical, verbal, emotional, sexual		
Workaholic		
Others (identify)		

Assess your own reality orientation

Are my expectations grounded on reality, or are they based on family of origin influences?

_____

_____

_____

_____

_____

_____

Are my current needs and desires influenced by unmet needs from my childhood?

_____

_____

_____

_____

_____

_____

Are my emotional expectations "normal," or, are they due to my family of origin experience?

_____

_____

_____

_____

_____

_____

_____

Spend 10 to 15 minutes (more time if needed) to share with each other your written responses to the exercises.

_____

_____

_____

_____

_____

_____

_____

_____

_____

_____

2) **Responsibility**—Your ability and willingness to be an equal partner in all aspects of your marital relationship are what define the uniqueness of your marriage.

Weigh your sense of responsibility: Respond Yes / No where it applies. Expand with your answer.

- As a youth, I was given age-appropriate responsibilities for myself/others.

  _____
  _____
  _____

- My parents enabled me 'to be a child' all throughout life.

  _____
  _____
  _____

- My childhood role contributed to the stability of my family of origin.

  _____
  _____
  _____

- My youthful responsibilities define me as an adult person.

  _____
  _____
  _____

- My parents influenced my adult attitude toward responsibility.

  _____
  _____
  _____

- My parent's influence applies to my sense of responsibility in my marriage.

  _____
  _____
  _____

- My behaviors demonstrate my effort to accept responsibilities in my marriage.

  _____
  _____
  _____

- My sense of responsibility provides direction to the life of my family.

  _____
  _____
  _____

Spend 10 to 15 minutes (more time if needed) to share with each other your written responses to the exercises.

_____

_____

_____

_____

_____

_____

_____

Failure to share the responsibilities in my marriage results in negative consequences and affects the harmony of my relationship with my spouse (family).

On a scale of 1 (low)—10 (high) how much do you share in each of the following responsibilities? Respond to the ones that apply to you.

	Myself	**My Spouse**
Finances		
Decision-making		
Self-care		
Household chores		
Emotional availability		
Parenting and childcare		
Structure/Disciplining the children		
Leisure activities		

How do the results of this exercise make you feel?

_____

_____

_____

_____

_____

What awareness did you gain from this exercise?

_____

_____

_____

_____

_____

Discuss what changes you want to make as a result of this exercise.

_____

_____

_____

_____

_____

Spend as much time as you need to share with each other your written responses to the exercises.

_____

_____

_____

_____

_____

_____

_____

_____

_____

3) **Relationships**—A person's relationships are grounded in their reality orientation, or it might be influenced by the family of origin orientation. The marriage is the arena for discerning the individual's part in the uniqueness of the relationship.

Self-assessment

- My most important goal in resolving conflicts with my spouse is...

  _____
  _____
  _____

- Are my responses to my spouse (or any situation) a re-enactment of my father's/mother's past actions/words?

  _____
  _____
  _____

- What prevents me from negotiating and compromising on issues when I'm in conflict with my spouse?

  _____
  _____
  _____

- What feelings, behaviors that were acceptable in my family of origin, which are now causing problems in my present relationship?

  _____
  _____
  _____

- What gets in the way of understanding my spouse's point of view when we are in conflict?

  _____
  _____
  _____

- What do I look for from my spouse to confirm that am I loved and valued?

  _____
  _____
  _____

Spend 10 to 15 minutes (more time if needed) to share with each other your written responses to the exercises.

_____

_____

_____

_____

_____

_____

_____

_____

_____

_____

CHAPTER 9

MULTIDIMENSIONAL ASPECTS OF MY MARRIAGE

Marriage may be compared to a plant that requires daily nurture, daily attention, daily care and cultivation. It will not develop of its own accord; only when effort and will are exerted will it grow and mature. For a marriage to succeed both husband and wife must be committed to its success. They must build an enduring love relationship that is centered in the heart of their consciousness. Their relationship must be nurtured with the water of loyalty and love.

—*Margaret Ruhe*

THE COMMITMENT TO THE multifaceted demands of marriage requires flexibility, openness, dedication and fortitude. The experience of confronting different but unifying roles in marriage requires willingness to be adaptable in an on-going learning process. For the individuals who are fulfilling their different roles in marriage, as a spouse and as a parent, the gains from the efforts are rewarding both personally, and socially in their contribution to building the future of the society.

You and the multidimensional aspects of your marriage

How willing are you to participate in the following areas of your marriage? [Score yourself from 1 to 10 with ten the highest possible rate.]

	Where I am now	**Where you want to be**
➤ Openness	_____	_____
➤ Intimacy	_____	_____
➤ Expression of feelings	_____	_____
➤ Sexual expression	_____	_____
➤ Spirituality	_____	_____
➤ Harmony	_____	_____
➤ Emotional engagement	_____	_____

With your spouse, explore your understanding and your willingness to participate in each item identified above. Be open to dialogue. Write down your thoughts.

Spend 10 to 15 minutes (more time if needed) to share with each other your written responses to the exercises.

_____

_____

_____

_____

_____

_____

Partnership in parental roles

Some couples maintain the façade of closeness as they publicly carry out their roles routinely as husband and wife and as parents. The legacy you choose for your children to have is conveyed in the way you participate in caring for them.

Description and importance of my parents as role models:

Description of what I learned through my experience from my role model of what I need to do to be a responsible parent:

Three Principles of Parenting

On a scale of 1–5 (high) rate your level of functioning in the following areas:

1) Generational boundary—I have the ability to create structure as a parent so that my children understand limits and respect for authority that will ensure their feeling of safety.

_____ I point out to my child(ren) unacceptable behaviors without demeaning them or shaming them.

2) Intentional parenting—As a parent I am clear in guiding my children with what I want them to become and what they can accomplish in their life as adults.

_____ I demonstrate how I feel toward my children by validating them for who they are in action and in words.

_____ I verbalize my appreciation about specific praiseworthy actions of my children.

_____ I convey to my spouse that we can be mutually supportive of our children.

3) Parental coalition—I value the importance of discussing family rules, concerns and activities with my spouse.

_____ I understand that my spouse and I need to work collaboratively in enforcing the rules and clearly communicating values to create a stable, peaceful and harmonious home environment.

Take turns 5 minutes each and discuss with your spouse your response to the above questions.

_____

_____

_____

_____

_____

Sexuality in Marriage

Human beings are meant to bond together. Apart from the bond between a parent and a child, there is no bond stronger than the bond in marriage. In marriage we make the vow for life. However, in many cases, couples drift apart and become emotionally disconnected, and sexually alienated.

Privately the feeling of being emotionally disconnected with each other is felt in the lack of intimacy and feeling of tenderness, specifically in the areas of communication and sexual relationship.

A strong bond in marriage does not happen spontaneously and naturally. It takes intentionality, a conscious decision to act in a certain way to achieve a needed result. The responsibility to make the bond strong lies on both partners, rooted in the belief that their marriage is important, and the care and love for each other are expressed.

Many of our beliefs, feelings and behaviors are learned from our family of origin. There are messages learned early in life that are related to sexuality and do become part of our outlook in life.

Respond to the following questions. They will help you to examine how your attitude/outlook is operational in your relationship with your spouse.

- How comfortable are you in initiating physical intimacy with your spouse?

  _____

  _____

  _____

- What thoughts and feelings do you have when you initiate sex with your spouse?

  _____

  _____

  _____

- In what circumstances or settings do you feel uncomfortable in being intimate with your spouse?

  _____

  _____

  _____

- How comfortable are you saying "no" to your spouse when he/she initiates sex?

  _____

  _____

  _____

○ What is the difference between you and your spouse in regards to your needs for physical intimacy? Frequency? Physical expression?

_____

_____

_____

○ What role does touching play in the expression of your physical intimacy toward each other?

_____

_____

_____

○ How aware are you of the positive or negative changes within yourself during sex with your spouse?

_____

_____

_____

○ Do you show feeling of tenderness toward your spouse? If your answer is "no," identify what is holding you back?

_____

_____

_____

On the scale of 0 to 5 (high) how often do you use sex:

_____ As a way of getting what you want from your spouse?

_____ As a way of creating distance between you and your spouse?

_____ As a way of creating closeness / intimacy?

How would you like your spouse to demonstrate to you physically that she/ he loves you? Explain.

_____

_____

_____

_____

_____

What is the role of sex in strengthening and maintaining the intimacy of your marriage? Explain

_____

_____

_____

_____

_____

What is the role of communication in strengthening and maintaining the intimacy of your marriage? Explain.

_____

_____

_____

_____

_____

What difficulties are you experiencing in your sexual relationship with your spouse? Explain.

_____

_____

_____

_____

How do you feel talking about sex with your spouse? Explain.

_____

_____

_____

_____

_____

How do you feel about your own sexuality? About sex itself? Explain.

_____

_____

_____

_____

_____

Has pornography been an issue between you and your spouse? Explain.

_____

_____

_____

_____

_____

As a result of your awareness, what specific changes are you willing to make to improve your sexual intimacy with your spouse? Explain

_____

_____

_____

_____

_____

Spend 10 to 15 minutes (more time if needed) to share with each other your written responses to the exercises.

_____

_____

_____

_____

_____

_____

_____

WRITE DOWN, SHARE AND EXPLORE WITH YOUR SPOUSE YOUR INSIGHT AND UNDERSTANDING OF YOUR OWN SEXUALITY.

Spirituality in marriage

Recognizing that the two people in marriage coming from different backgrounds, there is bound to be conflicts that need to be worked out. Prolonged and chronic issues could make the partners question their ability to continue their commitment to the marriage. For many of us, our beliefs help in maintaining our commitment. Reflect and expand your responses to the following questions:

During difficult times, what beliefs sustain me in my commitment to my marriage?

_____

_____

_____

_____

_____

How do my personal beliefs impact my own growth in the context of my marriage?

_____

_____

_____

_____

_____

What is the role of sex in my spiritual make up?

_____

_____

_____

_____

What is the role of communication with my spouse in my spirituality?

_____

_____

_____

_____

_____

What influence do my own beliefs and my spouse's beliefs have on our marriage?

_____

_____

_____

_____

_____

What do I understand about the rhythm of the ebb and flow of my own inner harmony and its impact on my marriage?

_____

_____

_____

_____

_____

What is the role of understanding and of acceptance in the strength of our marriage?

_____

_____

_____

_____

_____

What helps me to forgive and let go of past hurts in my marriage?

_____

_____

_____

_____

_____

How does my spouse's religious beliefs (or lack of beliefs), affect my marriage?

_____

_____

_____

_____

_____

What gives me hope for continuing my commitment to my marriage?

_____

_____

_____

_____

_____

Spend 10 to 15 minutes (more time if needed) to share with each other your written responses to the exercises.

_____

_____

_____

_____

_____

CHAPTER 10

MOVING FORWARD IN MY MARRIAGE

"In any relationship, there will be frightening spells in which your feelings of Love dry up. And when that happens you must remember that the essence of marriage is that it is a covenant, a commitment, a promise of future love. So what do you do? You do the acts of love, despite your lack of feeling. You may not feel tender, sympathetic, and eager to please, but in your actions you must BE tender, understanding, forgiving and helpful. And, if you do that as time goes on you will not only get through the dry spells, but they will become less frequent and deep, and you will become more constant in your feelings. This is what can happen if you decide to love."

—Timothy Keller

IT TAKES TWO EMOTIONALLY secure people to have a healthy relationship. Many of us look to our spouse to make us feel complete and wonderful. When this fails, in order to maintain the equilibrium in marriage, we learn to cope. We adjust who we are until it becomes intolerable, and we start drifting away from each other. _It is not necessary to lose and sacrifice who you are to save your marriage_.

The renewal of myself through the changes I make reinforces partnership in my marriage.

➢ How can I identify my own part in the equation of my marriage?

_____

_____

_____

➢ In what areas in my marriage do I set boundaries for myself in my relationship with my spouse?

_____

_____

_____

Describe how you demonstrate the importance of setting aside time to be together with your spouse to keep your marriage alive.

Work with your spouse to jointly decide to take the first step in enhancing your marriage. Describe the dynamics of this process.

In the area of communication rate the degree, 1 = low – 10 high, to which you are able to do the following with your spouse:

- _____ initiate a dialogue
- _____ share insights
- _____ share pain
- _____ self-discovery
- _____ self-disclose voluntarily

Spend 10 to 15 minutes (more time if needed) to share with each other your written responses to the exercises.

_____

_____

_____

_____

_____

_____

_____

_____

_____

_____

_____

_____

_____

_____

_____

Write notes to yourself about your insights; and about your feelings and thoughts about your insights.

Resolve issues before they become chronic or a crisis

All the effort put forth in the application of this workbook brought firmer commitment to maintaining and in further strengthening your marriage. Being sensitive to the subtlety of self-deception is a way to avoid slipping back to the behavioral patterns that will sabotage the work that you have done so far toward growth of your marriage.

The awareness and insights you have gained about yourself are valuable in an ongoing evaluation of how you want your marriage to be.

- Triggers—for myself?
  - for my spouse?
- Signs—for myself?
  - for my spouse?

What are the warning signs when something is going wrong in my relationship with my spouse?

With myself?

With my spouse?

What action do I take to diffuse a conflict that has a potential to escalate?

With myself?

With my spouse?

Spend 10 to 15 minutes (more time if needed) to share with each other your written responses to the exercises.

In life we will always encounter situations that can potentially turn into a problem. A situation becomes a problem when we deal with it ineffectively. It continues to be a problem when we do not know how to solve it, or, unwilling to take action to deal with it by getting help with someone who might provide some guidance in dealing with the problem. Therefore, the problem is not the issue; it is how a person deals with the situation that turns it into a problem.

Rate the frequency, 1 (low)—10 (high), when the statements below are applied IN YOUR INTERACTION with your spouse with <u>an issue/conflict</u> that is not HEALTHY and that is in fact, TOXIC.

_____ When the issue is focused on attacking the person and not the behavior.

_____ When the issue is part of unresolved past conflict that is not within the control of either party, and either one person or both are not able to let go.

_____ When the couple is unable to come to a compromise regarding an issue and cannot accept that they are in disagreement.

_____ When a family member of a spouse is used in a derogatory manner to make a point.

_____ When the knowledge you have about your spouse is used against him/her.

_____ When the view of the current issue is linked with past event.

_____ When confusing emotion with reason.

_____ When conclusion is made based on assumption about a situation, or about your spouse.

_____ (Others)—Describe.

Style of Communication—Rate 1 (low)—10 (high) Myself

	Myself	My Spouse
Connecting—communication that focuses on self-responsibility		
Distancing—Communication is focused on your spouse' behavior and thinking		

Discuss with your spouse the consequences of the pattern of your interaction. And if no change takes place, discuss what would be the long term consequence for your marriage?

Issues and conflict resolution—Respond "yes" or "no" based on how well you follow the communication guideline:

_____ **Are you able to define the problem?**

_____ **Are you able to set aside your issue, anger and "ego" in order to listen to the words, the tone, and the meaning of your spouse?**

_____ **Are you able to focus on current issue?**

Example

Negative = You're doing it again…always…

Positive = I am really upset over what you are doing / saying. Please explain to me so I can understand.

_____ **Are you able to clarify what your spouse is saying? Positive = I hear you say…**

Conflict Resolution skills—Respond "yes" or "no" to the following:

_____ Are you able to take responsibility for yourself without blaming your spouse, parents or others?

Example:

Negative = You make me feel…

Positive = I feel…

_____ Are you able to avoid 'cross-talk' (talk about yourself and not about your spouse)?

Example

Negative = You need to look at…

Positive = I need help. How can we work on this?

_____ Are you able to practice active listening, to paraphrase and to confirm?

Positive = I want to understand. Are you saying…

Spend 10 to 15 minutes (more time if needed) to share with each other your written responses to the exercises.

_____

_____

_____

_____

_____

_____

_____

_____

_____

_____

Diffuse potentially toxic situations—Rate your level of action, 1 = low—5 = high in implementing the following:

_____ Your ability to disengage when conflict threatens to escalate to a destructive level.

_____ Your willingness to agree on a time to re-engage.

_____ Your willingness to set an immediate time frame to achieve closure or to move toward resolution.

_____ Your ability to take responsibility for self-soothing, such as calming yourself down with self-talk, walking, writing, etc.

_____ Your ability and willingness to re-engage when both parties are cool, calm and collected.

   o _____ Restate the initial position

   o _____ Explore underlying concerns

   o _____ Pursue creative solutions that address the concerns

_____ Your ability and willingness to make every effort to understand your partner without being judgmental.

Write notes to yourself about your insights; and about your feelings and thoughts about your insights. Spend 10 to 15 minutes (more time if needed) to share with spouse.

CHAPTER 11

KEEPING THE COMMITMENT ALIVE

Forgiveness is not about forgetting…it is about letting go. To forgive is to release you from your pain. Forgiveness does not establish relationship…unless people speak the truth about what they have done…change their mind and behavior, a relationship of trust is not possible. When you forgive someone…you release them from judgment, but without true change, no real relationship can be established. Forgiveness… offers an opportunity for reconciliation.

—*WM. Paul Young, The Shack*

Love is a decision—*It is a deliberate and an intentional process.* Both individuals need to recognize their contribution in making the marriage a growing experience. Differences and conflicts between two people are inevitable; we need to accept this reality.

Identify the words/attitude you use or you have when you communicate with your spouse. Rate the strength of your feelings 1—10, 10 being more intense. Do the same thing for your spouse: identify and rate the validating and invalidating words/ attitudes used.

Validating/connecting words/attitude   Invalidating/distancing words/attitudes

Myself / My spouse   **Myself / My spouse**

_____/ _____ affection   _____/ _____ anger

_____/ _____ concern   _____/ _____ fear

_____/ _____ joy   _____/ _____ mistrust

_____/ _____ interest   _____/ _____ disgust

_____/ _____ positive regard   _____/ _____ belligerence

_____/ _____ partnership   _____/ _____ dominance

_____/ _____ support   _____/ _____ blame

_____/ _____ validation   _____/ _____ criticism

_____/ _____ kindness   _____/ _____ defensiveness

_____/ _____ passion   _____/ _____ complaint

_____/ _____ generosity   _____/ _____ coldness

Score each side. If the side of invalidating/distancing words has a higher score, circle the ones you can prioritize to work on. Describe how you would make the changes.

Describe how you would maintain the application of the <u>validating/connecting words / attitudes</u> in your emotional interaction with your spouse to enhance your marriage.

Spend 10 to 15 minutes (more time if needed) to share with each other your written responses to the exercises.

_____

_____

_____

_____

_____

_____

_____

_____

_____

_____

_____

_____

_____

_____

How do I mend my marriage?

The healing process of a marriage is based upon the following premises:

- **As a spouse, I share the responsibility in the success and failure of my marriage.**

  What responsibility have I assumed in this marriage? How does it help or hinder the marriage?

  _____

  _____

  _____

  How does my sense of self-righteousness cause conflict in my marriage?

  _____

  _____

  _____

  How does my lack of understanding of my spouse contribute to our problems?

  _____

  _____

  _____

- **Marriage is not a competition, it is a partnership.**

  What strengths do I bring into this marriage to complement my partner's strength?

  _____

  _____

  _____

  How do I show that I am motivated and that I trust myself to work on our marriage?

  _____

  _____

  _____

  How much do I trust my spouse to work on our marriage?

  _____

  _____

  _____

- **As a spouse I have the responsibility to monitor myself.**

  What words / phrases / attitude do I consistently use to relate to my spouse?

  _____

  _____

  _____

  What message is relayed by my body language/facial expressions?

  _____

  _____

  _____

  What is the tone of my voice?

  _____

  _____

  _____

  Do I just hear or am I really listening to what my spouse has to say?

  _____

  _____

  _____

  Do I allow myself to feel vulnerable by talking about my feelings and about myself with my spouse?

  _____

  _____

  _____

What actions or words of my spouse trigger reactions in me? Positive/Negative?

_____
_____
_____

What are my thoughts and feelings behind these reactions?

_____
_____
_____

Are these thoughts, feelings, reactions reality-based, or are they are coming from my family of origin?

_____
_____
_____

- **As a spouse what behaviors can I identify that gratify my own needs at the expense of my spouse and my marriage?**
  List specific behaviors that cause conflict between my spouse and me.

_____
_____
_____

Discuss with your spouse the behaviors you have identified and agree upon one behavior you can both start to work on.

_____
_____
_____

What type of support can we agree on that will help me/us in our efforts to change?

_____
_____
_____

What first step can I take to help me internalize the change I need to make?

_____
_____
_____

Spend 10 to 15 minutes (more time if needed) to share with each other your written responses to the exercises.

_____

_____

_____

_____

_____

_____

_____

_____

_____

_____

_____

_____

_____

Rate your sensitivity towards your spouse. On a scale of 1—10 (high) rate yourself in the following areas:

_____ communicating my perceptions of the feelings and concerns of my spouse.

_____ sharing my recognition of the verbal and non-verbal feelings, needs and concerns of my spouse.

_____ anticipating and sharing the emotional effects of my spouse's specific behavior toward me.

_____ re-stating my understanding of my spouse's point of view and asking for feedback concerning my accuracy.

_____ my being aware when I am shutting down my spouse.

_____ being aware when I am shutting out my spouse.

_____ purposely (or unconsciously) hurting my spouse with my words and actions.

Write down what you have experienced and insights you gained from this exercise.

Hold a dialogue with your spouse sharing internal conflicts and discomforts: ask for feedback from your spouse.

What feedback did you get from your spouse and how helpful is it to you?

THE 4 F'S OF MAINTAINING MY MARRIAGE

Rate 1 = low–10 = high your level of awareness and your intentionality in maintaining the following:

	Now	Goal
➤ **Being FAITHFUL**	_____	_____
○ making the commitment to the exclusivity of my marriage	_____	_____
○ recognizing and accepting the demands of my marriage	_____	_____
➤ **Being FORGIVING**	_____	_____
○ accepting the hurt and the feeling of being wronged by my spouse	_____	_____
○ letting go of the anger and resentment	_____	_____
➤ **Being FLEXIBLE**	_____	_____
○ accepting the changes in my marriage	_____	_____
○ supporting my spouse's development	_____	_____
○ accommodating the needs of others, such as our children	_____	_____
➤ **Being FUN**	_____	_____
○ joyful companionship	_____	_____
○ united in mutual interests	_____	_____
○ create enjoyable activities	_____	_____

Write notes to yourself about your insights; and also about feelings and thoughts about your insights.

Spend 10 to 15 minutes (more time if needed) to share with each other your written responses to the exercises.

_____

_____

_____

_____

_____

_____

_____

_____

_____

_____

_____

_____

_____

_____

_____

CHAPTER 12

PREVENTING THE RETURN TO OLD BEHAVIORS AND ATTITUDES

We are told that people stay in love because of chemistry, or because they remain intrigued with Each Other, or because of luck….. but part of it has got to be forgiveness and gratefulness.

—Ellen Goodman

MARRIAGES FAIL WHEN WE give up due to the frustration of repeated setbacks and the perception that nothing will change. It is difficult to forget the many years of buried pains and confusion that makes us alienated from ourselves and our own best interests. Relapse could lead us back to the feeling of isolation and disconnectedness. To prevent that cycle, we strengthen our commitment by "acting as if…" until the new behavior is internalized. This experience becomes self-rewarding due to the realization and the efficacy of self-empowerment: the feeling that "I can do it." And that feeling is reinforced by positive responses we receive from our spouse.

Preventing the cycle

Rate 1—10 (high)—Identify indicators of tendency to relapse.

1) Your level of awareness of the signals of your tendency to relapse.
2) The level of effort you apply in changing toward the desired behaviors.

A—Situations that would trigger relapse to old behaviors. Describe your triggers.

_____ Level of awareness of the signals

_____ Level of effort applied in changing to the desired behaviors.

B—Specific negative feelings and behaviors that you feel drawn to go back to.

_____ Level of awareness of the signals

_____ Level of effort applied in changing to the desired behaviors.

C. Reason for resistance in implementing the new behaviors.

_____ Level of effort applied in changing to the desired behaviors.

_____ Level of effort applied in changing to the desired behaviors.

If you are not where you think you should be, what level would you like to aim for, and in which areas, A), B) C) ?

Name the new behaviors that will facilitate significant change in your marriage.

Write down what you will do about it?

_____

_____

_____

_____

_____

_____

_____

Share with your spouse the level of awareness you gained from this exercise and the rate of your level the motivation to change.

_____

_____

_____

_____

_____

_____

_____

Be open to giving and receiving feedback.

_____

_____

_____

_____

_____

_____

_____

_____

OOPS, I DID IT AGAIN

Emotional relapse: Going back to familiar habits even though you are aware of the negative consequences. Answer the following questions:

What makes it difficult for me to stay on track?

What is behind my resistance to change?

What experiences from my family of origin block my growth in my marriage?

What am I willing to do to continue the process of change?

Self-monitoring for warning signals of relapse. Rate yourself 1 (low) to 5(high)

_____ Gradual drifting into my old patterns

_____ Insensitivity to my spouse's concerns

_____ Unwillingness to evaluate my thinking and feeling in relation to my behavior

_____ My personal needs being placed in higher priority over the need of my marriage

_____ Omitting important disclosures with my spouse

_____ Having the attitude of not caring

Spend 10 to 15 minutes (more time if needed) to share with each other your written responses to the exercises.

_____

_____

_____

_____

_____

"Marriage is a commitment- a decision to do, all through life, that which will express your love for one's spouse."

—Herman H. Kieval

Dealing with a relapse

Rate yourself 1 to 10 (high)—If you are not on the level where you want to be, what can you do to get to where you want to be? State your plan of action for each one.

_____ Self-examine—(plan of action)

_____ Disclose—(plan of action)

_____ Communicate openly—(plan of action)

_____ Hear and listen—(plan of action)

_____ Receive feedback—(plan of action)

_____ Accept feedback—(plan of action)

_____ Understand—(plan of action)

_____ Forgive—(plan of action)

_____ Continue to search out reason to continue your love more deeply—(plan of action)

LOVING, FORGIVING AND ACCEPTING

The success and failure of my marriage depends on forgiving my spouse and myself for the disappointments I experience in our marriage.

I recognize my share in the responsibility for making my marriage work; I am willing to collaborate in this effort.

I am making a deliberate decision to continue to love my spouse.

I affirm the above statements.

Name: _____

Date: _____

"Love is patient. Love is kind. Love does not envy. Love does not boast. Love is not proud. Love is not rude. Love is not self-seeking. Love is not easily angered. Love keeps no record of wrongs. Love does not delight in evil. Love rejoices with the truth. Love always protects. Love always trusts. Love always hopes. Love always perseveres. Love never fails."

—1 Corinthians 13: 4-8

CHAPTER 13

RE-EVALUATING THE FOUNDATIONS OF THE STRENGTH OF MY MARRIAGE

THE TREE REPRESENTS THE years of having survived the natural elements of life. As in marriage, the years of challenges in life provided the foundation for a strong marriage. Dave Meurer, an author, stated that a great marriage is not when the "perfect couple" comes together. It is when an imperfect couple learns to enjoy their differences.

Your journey in exploring the roots of your marriage leads you to rediscover who you are in the intimacy of the most important person in your life, your spouse, and it leads you to your growth together in marriage.

Post-Screening:

Name: _____ Spouse: _____

Date: _____

RELATIONSHIPS SKILLS

At the completion of this workbook re-evaluate and rate the skills gained and demonstrated in the relationships in yourself and your spouse. Rank each area: 1 = low – 10 = high.

	Spouse	Self

Self-management—the ability to deal with stressful situations using the skills below:

	Spouse	Self
Self-talk		
Self-understanding		
Self-care		
Self-esteem		

Relationships—the level of comfort and connection made in these different contexts:

	Spouse	Self
Intra-personal		
Inter-personal		
Family		
Friends		

Feelings—the ability to identify emotions, its source and how it is expressed in action.

	Spouse	Self
Understanding		
Expressive		
Connecting feeling with behavior		

Communication—being aware of the effect on others the way one communicates.

	Spouse	Self
Distancing		
Connecting		
Style		
Assertive		
Aggressive		

Passive		
Passive/aggressive		

Listening—being attentive in communication, and in being open in receiving and giving feedback.

Active		
Feedback		
Giving		
Receiving		

Share with your spouse the level of awareness you gained from this exercise. Be open to giving and receiving feedback.

Post-Screening:

Name: _____ Spouse: _____

Date: _____

THE FRAMEWORK OF YOUR BEHAVIOR IN RELATIONSHIP

At the completion of the workbook re-evaluate and rate the skills gained and demonstrated in the relationships in yourself and your spouse. Rank each area: 1 = low—10 = high.

	Spouse	Self

Relationship—connection of the couple is operationally expressed in the following areas:

Intimacy		
Openness		
Expression of feelings		
Emotional engagement		

Responsibility—the couple functions as equal partners. Imbalanced shows in either action below:

Enabling		
Control		

Reality Orientation—the ability to stay in the "here and now" to assess situations.

Impulsivity		
Isolation		
Shame		
Guilt		

Escapism—inability to remain grounded in reality to focus on what is of value in the relationship.

Substance abuse		
Workaholism		
Gambling		
Sex—pornography, infidelity (specify)		
Other (specify)		

Abuse—misuse of power that degrades the other person.

Physical		
Verbal		
Emotional		
Sexual		

Commitment—valuing the permanency of the relationship.

Motivation		
Determination		
Inner harmony		

Share with your spouse the level of awareness you gained from this exercise. Be open to giving and receiving feedback.

Post-Screening:

Name: _____ Spouse: _____

Date: _____

ELEMENTS OF A LOVING RELATIONSHIP

At the completion of the workbook re-evaluate and rate the skills gained and demonstrated in the relationships in yourself and your spouse with minuses and plusses.

The Elements	Self	Spouse
Commitment—promises exclusivity		
Sees good in the relationship		
Values the investment in the relationship		
Values the identity as a couple		
Aware of part in the problem		
Intimacy—values emotional closeness		
Sees good in self and spouse		
Affirms the value of the other person		
Appreciates the other person's action		
Affection is shown verbally and physically		
Caring—shows concern for another's welfare		
Trustworthy		
Reliable		
Protective—maintains integrity as a couple		
Spends meaningful time as a couple		
Enjoyment—as individuals & as a couple		
Negotiates activities that are pleasurable		
Initiates enjoyable activities		
Responsibility—accepts share of problems		
Accepts interdependence in the relationship		
Does not blame others		
Sharing hurt—in order to find a solution		

Recognizes that anger masks other feelings		
Looks at pattern of hurtful behavior		
Examines the source of hurtful behavior		
Forgiveness—acceptance and understanding		
Validates hurt in self and partner		
Recognizes unforgiven hurts = resentment		
Passion—affection, longing, sexual intimacy		
Shares likes and dislikes		
Spontaneous		

Share with your spouse the level of awareness you gained from this exercise. Be open to giving and receiving feedback.

APPENDICES

CHECKLIST:
CHAPTERS / DATE COMPLETED

DYNAMICS OF MARRIAGE: "THE Family of Origin" Approach Workbook

Name:

Date:

Introduction										
1—Elements of a healthy marriage										
2—Assessment of my marriage skills and its bases										
3—Communication COUPLE'S THERAPY AGREEMENT										
4—The accountability I bring to my marriage										
5—Reacquainting myself with my past experiences										
6—Understanding the legacy of my family of origin										
7—Learning more about me in the context of my marriage										
8—Uniqueness of my marriage										
9—Multi-dimensional aspects of my marriage										
10—Moving forward on my marriage										
11—Keeping the commitment alive										
12—My marriage: preventing the return of my old behaviors										
13—Re-evaluating the foundations of the strength of my marriage										

Comments:

TERMINATION
INTERVIEW QUESTIONS

Describe your experience through the therapeutic process of understanding the legacy of the roots of your marriage.

_____

_____

_____

_____

_____

How much of your understanding of the influence of your family of your origin helped you in working through the problems in your marriage in this therapy? Describe.

_____

_____

_____

_____

_____

What was the most significant discovery you have made about yourself through marriage therapy?

_____

_____

_____

_____

_____

How would rate your marriage from 1= low – 10 = high:

_____ before therapy

_____ after therapy

_____

_____

_____

_____

_____

Would you be interested in follow-up / maintenance therapy on a regular or on occasional basis either by phone or in person?

_____

_____

_____

_____

_____

If your answer is yes, please provide me with your email address, or you can contact me through my email address: Leticia@dynamicsofmarriage.com

Name: _____

email address: _____

Signature: _____

Date: _____

SIGNIFICANCE OF TERMS

Boundary: Setting limit within oneself and between self and others.

Control: Inability to let go or to allow others to take responsibility for their thoughts and actions.

Emotional abuse: Behaviors that cause emotional suffering such as ignoring, verbal abuse, criticism.

Emotional disengagement: Being emotionally un-affected by another person or by events.

Enabling: Being overly responsible for another person so that he/ she avoids self-responsibility.

Escapism: A tendency to ward off unpleasant feelings by addictive/ compulsive behavior, or by other avoidance maneuvers such as fantasizing, sleeping, overworking, overeating, etc.

Excessive guilt: Feeling guilty for things one is not responsible for. Feeling guilty to an inappropriate degree for a wrong doing.

Expression of feelings: Outwardly communicating one's feelings.

Family of origin: The group of people who played significant roles in your upbringing.

Identity: Your knowledge of yourself as a person and a sense of who you are that comes from within.

Impulsivity: Acting without understanding why or without evaluating the consequences of the action.

Intentional behavior: Conscious decision to behave in a certain way to achieve a desired result.

Intimacy: Mutual sharing of closeness (emotional, sexual, etc.)

Isolation: Lack of interpersonal connection with others.

Nuclear family: Made up of parents and children.

Openness: Being appropriately honest about one's feeling; willingness to respect other's feelings and point of view.

Physical abuse: Physically harmful actions: pushing, hitting, choking, etc.

Responsible: Taking ownership for thoughts, feelings, actions and accepting the consequences.

Role: The part you play in a relationship.

Sexual abuse: Inappropriate sexual behavior. May be forced and may include touching, voyeurism, exhibiting sexual organs, etc. May be unforced (such as compliance by a child); any sexual behavior between an adult in a position of authority or power over a child or person under their care.

Shame-based feelings: Perceiving and feeling "self" as being different, worthless and inadequate.

SUGGESTED READINGS

Barker, P. *Basic Family Therapy*. New York: Oxford University International Press, 1986.

Boss, E., & Davis, L. *The Courage to Heal*. New York: Harper and Row Publishers, 1988.

Bradshaw, J. *Healing the Shame That Binds You*. Deerfield Beach: Health Communication, Inc., 1988.

Forward, S. *Emotional Blackmail*. New York: Harper Collins Publishers, Inc., 1997.

Forward, S. *Toxic Parents*. New York: Bantam Books, 1989.

Framo, J.L. *Family of Origin Therapy*. New York: Brunner/ Mazel Inc. 1992.

Gottman, J., Notarius, C., Gonso, J., & Markman, H. *A Couple's Guide to Communication*. Champaign, Illinois: Research Press, 1976.

Kutz, E. Shame and Guilt, Hazelden, 1976.

Lobsennz, N. & Weinsinger, H. *Nobody's Perfect*. Los Angeles: Stratford Press, 1981.

Marlin, E. *Genograms*. Chicago: Contemporary Books, 1989.

Miller, A. *For Your Own Good*. New York: Straus, Giroux, 1983.

Paine-Gernee, K & Hunt, T. *Emotional Healing*. New York: Waener Books, Inc., 1990.

Richardson, R. *Family ties that Bind*. Canada: International Self Press, 1984.

Whitfield, C. *A Gift to Myself*. Deerfield Beach: Health Communications Inc., 1990.

Woititz, J.G. *Adult Children Of Alcoholics*. Pompano Beach: Health Communications Inc., 1983.

REFERENCES

Avakame, Edem F. (1998). Intergenerational transmission of violence and psychological aggression against wives. Canadian Journal of Behavioural Science. Ottawa: Vol. 30.

Barbara Józefik, Maciej Wojciech Pilecki (2010) Perception of autonomy and intimacy in families of origin of patients with eating disorders with depressed patients and healthy controls. A Transgenerational perspective—Part I Process; Archives of Psychiatry.

Buchbinder, Eli, Goldblatt, Hadass. (2010). <u>Shattered Vision: Disenchantment of Couplehood Among Female Survivors of Violence in the Shadow of their Family-of-Origin Experience.</u> Journal Interpersonal Violence.

Celano, Marianne P., Smith, C. O., Kaslow, N. J. (2010) A Competency-Based Approach to Couple and Family Therapy Supervision. Psychotherapy Theory. Research Practice. Training. Vol 47.

Dean M Busby; Brandt C Gardner; Narumi Taniguchi. (2005). The Family of Origin Parachute Model: Landing Safely in Adult Romantic Relationships. Family Relations Research Library.

Dean M Busby; Brandt C Gardner. (2008). How do I Analyze Thee? Let Me Count the Ways: Considering Empathy in Couple Relationships Using Self and Partner Ratings. Family Process; Research Library.

Dean M Busby; David C Ivey; Steven M Harris; Chance Ates. (2007). Self Directed, Therapist-Directed, and Assessment-Based Interventions for Premarital Couples.

Dean M Busby; Thomas B Holman; Eric Walker. (2008) Pathways to Relationship Aggression Between Adult Partners. Family Relations. Research Library.

Dean M Busby; Thomas B Holman; Sylvia Niehuis. (2009). The Association Between Partner Enhancement and Self-Enhancement and Relationship Quality Outcomes. Journal of Marriage and Family.

Dean M Busby; Thomas B Holman. (2009). Perceived Match or Mismatch on the Gottman Conflict Styles: Associations with relationship outcomes variables. Family Archives of Psychiatry and Psychotherapy, 2010; 4.

Dinero, Rachel E., Conger, Rand D., Shaver, Philip R., Widaman, Keith F., Larsen-Rife, Dannelle. (2009). Influence of Family of origin and Adult Romantic Partners on Attachment Security. J Family Psychology 22. Family Relations; Research Library.

Froma, Walsh. (1993) Normal Family Processes. New York, NY: The Guilford Press.

Gardner, Brandt C., Busby, Dean M., Brimball, Andrew S. (2007). Putting Emotional Reactivity in It's Place? Exploring Family of Origin Influences on Emotional Reactivity, Conflict, and Satisfaction in Premarital Couples. Contemporary Family Therapy 29

Gurman, Alan S., Kniskern, David P (1991) Handbook of Family Therapy Volume 11. New York, NY: Brunner/ Mazel Inc.

Hardy, Kenneth V., Laszloffy, Tracey A. (1995). The Cultural Genogram: Key to training culturally competent family therapist. Oxford: Vol. 21

Jason S Carroll; William J Doherty. (2003). Evaluating the effectiveness of premarital prevention programs: A meta-analytic review of outcome research. Family Relations; Research Library.

Jill D Duba. (2009). The Basic Needs Genogram: A Tool to Help Inter-Religious Couples Negotiate. International Journal of Reality Therapy. Highland Park:. Vol. 29, Iss. 1, Psychotherapy, Research Library

Julie Hatfield Boston Globe. (1995). Genogram: Therapy in Short Form. Daily News. Los Angeles, California.p.

Larson, Jeffry H., Mark J. Benson, Stephan M. Wilson, and Nilufer Medora. (1998). Family of origin influences on marital attitudes and readiness for marriage in late adolescents. Journal of Family Issues. 19.n6 (Nov): 750(19).

Shoshana Bulow. (2009). Integrating Sex and Couples Therapy: A Multifaceted Case History. Family Process. Oxford:Sep. Vol. 48.

Simpson, Jeffry A, Collins, Andrew, Tran, Sisi & Haydon, Katherine (2007). Attachment and the Experience of Emotions in Romantic Relationships: A Developmental Perspective. Journal of Personality and Social Psychology Vol. 92

Smith,Travis (2011). Understanding Infidelity: An Interview with Gerald Weeks. The Family Journal: Counseling and Therapy for Couples and Families. DOI 10.1177/106648011405445.

Snyder, Douglas k., Cozzi, Jebber J., Grich, Jami, Luebbert, Michael C. The Tapestry of Couple Therpy: Interveaving Theory, Assessment, and Intervention.

Sporakowski, Michael J. (1995). Assessment and Diagnosis in Marriage and Family Counseling. Journal of Counseling & Development. V 74

Steinberg, S. J., Davila, J., Fincham, F. (2005). Adolescent Marital Expectations and Romantic Experiences: Associations With Perceptions About Parental Conflict and Adolescent Attachment Security. Journal of Youth and Adolescence. Vol 35. No 3.

Wample, K.S., Shi, L., Nelson, B. S., Kimball, T. G. (2003) Families & family interviews, Intergenerational relationships Therapy. Family Process. Oxford: Vol. 42

Yelsma, P., Hovestadt, A. J., Anderson, W. T., Nilsson, J. E.,(2000). Family-of-origin expressiveness: Measurement meaning and relationship to Alexithymia. Journal of Marital and Family Therapy.

ABOUT THE AUTHOR

Mrs. Leticia S. Isidro-Clancy received her Master's degree from New York University. She is a Licensed Professional Counselor-Marriage and Family Therapist, a Licensed Clinical Alcohol and Drug Counselor in the State of New Jersey, nationally certified as Master Addiction Counselor, trained in and practices EMDR and a Certified Clinical Supervisor.

When on Staff at Fort Belvoir Community Hospital in Child/ Adolescent Behavioral Health, Ms. Isidro-Clancy provided therapy to families, couples and individuals, in both group and individual modalities. She was a Clinical Staff for the Army Substance Abuse Program in Army Posts in Europe and in SHAPE, Belgium. She also facilitated Couples groups for parishioners at SHAPE Belgium. She had been a Staff for the Navy Substance Abuse Prevention Program in Naples, Italy and a Program Coordinator for the Program at the Naval Training Center in Orlando, Florida. Prior to being part of the DOD staff Behavioral Health Service, she had been program coordinator for both for Catholic Charities and later for Carrier Foundation in New Jersey.

She has been an International Presenter; to the U.S. Army Europe Surgical Medical- Behavioral Science Conference, Willigen, Germany, and to the Chaplains and Chaplains' Assistants for the Family Life Office in Wurzburg, Germany. She has presented to the Annual Conference for the International Association of Marriage and Family Therapist (IAMFT), Northampton University in England, and to the Annual Conference of the European Branch of American Counseling Association (EBACA) in Willigen, Germany.

Mrs. Isidro-Clancy was a presenter/ facilitator for weekly follow up sessions to the Retrouvaille Program for couples in the Diocese of Trenton, NJ. An instructor for the University of La Verne in Naples, Italy, she has also taught both lower and upper level courses in Counseling and Psychology. She provided seminars to The Family Service Centers, to the Group of Military Wives in Naples, Italy, and to the U.S. Embassy and St Stephens International School in Rome, Italy.

Mrs. Isidro-Clancy was the Founder/Director of the Children Center in Naples, Italy. The Center, was a Parents' Co-Op Day School/Nursery-Day Care, which operated for over 25 years, provided services to support and enhance the quality of life for NATO and the U.S. military families in the area.

Mrs. Isidro-Clancy has published another book, *Exploring the Roots of Your Marriage, Understanding the Influence of the Family of Origin.*

www.ingramcontent.com/pod-product-compliance
Lightning Source LLC
Chambersburg PA
CBHW080623030426
42336CB00018B/3061

Repeat rows: 1-8.

Bind off after the last row 8 as follows: Slip the edge stitch onto the right needle, knit the next 1, then insert the left needle through the slipped edge stitch, from left to right, and pass it over the knitted stitch, *now there is 1 stitch on the right needle, knit the next 1 (now there are 2 stitches on the right needle), insert the left needle through the 1st stitch on the right needle, from left to right, and pass it over the 2nd one* repeat from * to * until the end of the row.

Cast on a multiple of 18, plus 3 and 2 edge stitches. Eighteen-stitch repeat. Repeat rows: 1-8. **The edge stitches are not included in the description below and must be added. Slip the first edge stitch, purl the last one.**

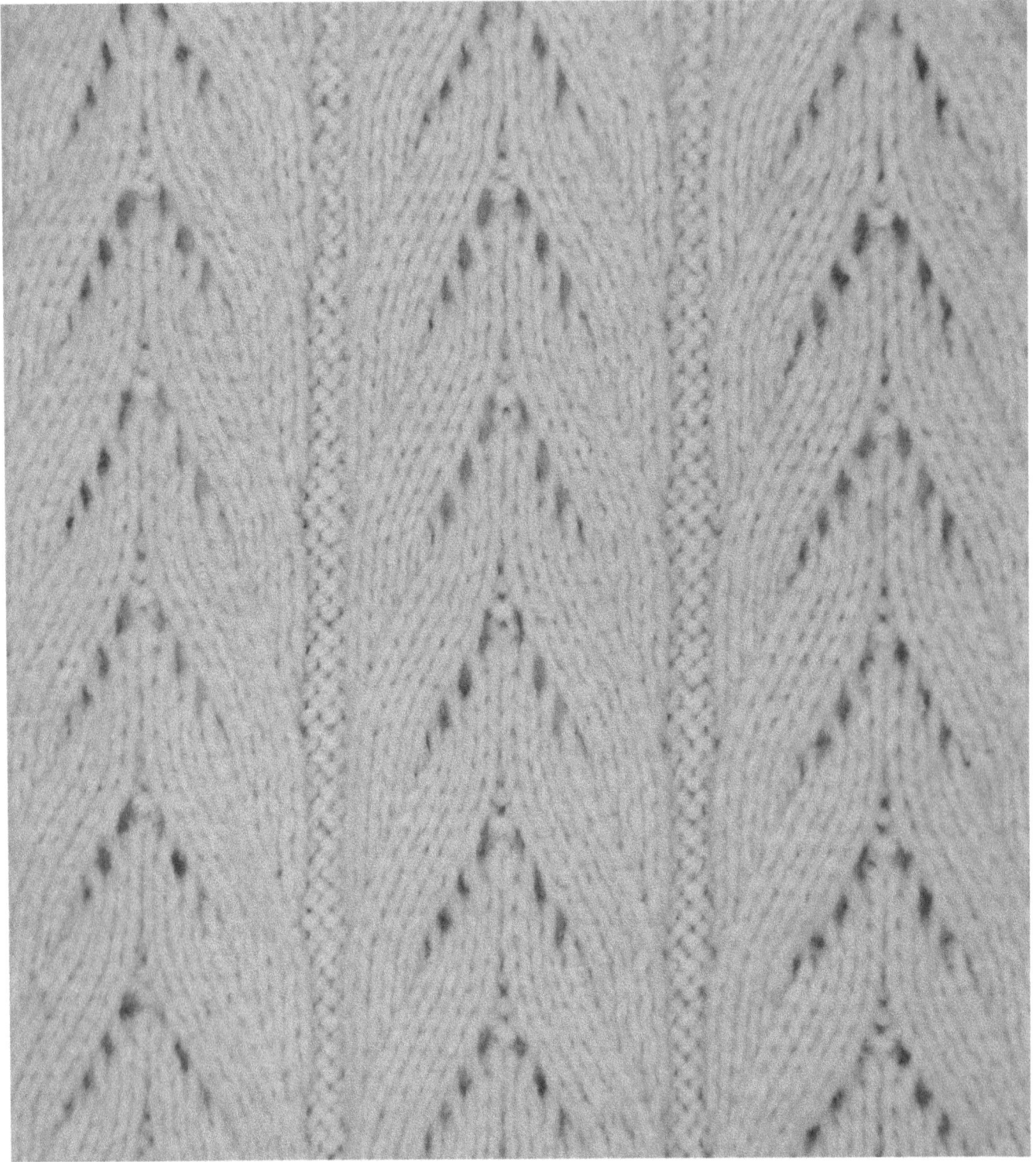

Pattern 44